A Commentary on the Bible

Leviticus
Numbers
&
Deuteronomy

by
Jeanne Guyon

Leviticus, Numbers,& Deuteronomy
All *new* material in this edition
copyrighted by SeedSowers Publishing House
Printed in the United States of America
All rights reserved

Published by SeedSowers Publishing House
                  P.O. Box 3317
                  Jacksonville, Fl 32206
                  1-800-228-2665
                  www.seedsowers.com

Library of Congress Cataloging - in - Data
          Guyon, Jeanne
          Leviticus, Numbers, Deuteronomy / Jeanne Guyon
          ISBN 0-940232-90-1
          1. Commentary

Times New Roman 12 pt.

Table of Contents

Book I

LEVITICUS

WITH REFLECTIONS REGARDING THE DEEPER CHRISTIAN LIFE.

CHAPTER I.

8. And the priests, Aaron's sons, shall lay the parts, the head and the fat, in order upon the wood that is on the fire which is upon the altar.

9. But the inwards and the legs shall he wash in water; and the priests shall burn them upon the altar, to be a burnt-offering of a sweet savor unto the Lord.

All these sacrifices of the law are the figures of interior sacrifices, as the apostles themselves have declared (I Peter ii. 5; Eph. V.2.). But there are several kinds of them, and in all, the creature always reserves something to itself, according as it was figured in those of the law, in which a part of what had been offered to God was laid aside for the priests and Levites. Such are the sacrifices of all the active and passive states, and even the mystic ones at their commencement. There is only the state of pure sacrifice, represented by the burnt-offering, which retains nothing and burns everything, even what seemed most necessary for the subsistence of the proper life; and it is this pure sacrifice which forms the consummation of the mystic state.

3

CHAPTER IX.

22. And Aaron came down from offering the sin-offering, the burnt-offering, and the peace offerings.

All that man can perform for himself is to offer victims; and for others, to sacrifice them and lay them in order, bringing to them, as a priest, the fire of charity. This being done, he has exhausted all that lies in his power, and must *come down* again into himself to allow God to act.

24. And there came a fire out from before the Lord and consumed the burnt-offering and the fat that were upon the altar, which when all the people saw, they praised the Lord, and fell upon their faces.

But when the soul has arrived at a certain state of purity, God *sends forth a devouring fire* from His countenance, that is to say from Himself, who is perfect charity; and this fire *consumes the burnt-offering*, burning all that remained of himself in the man, destroying it, and reducing it to ashes: and this is the consummation of perfect annihilation, which can only be wrought by God Himself, and by the fire of His countenance, which is the purest and most disinterested love.

CHAPTER X.

1. The two sons of Aaron, Nadab and Abihu, took each of them his censer, and put fire therein, and incense thereon, and offered a strange fire before the Lord.

God is so jealous of His glory and pure love, that He cannot suffer a *strange fire*, such as is not kindled upon His altar, that is, in Himself. There is no middle point; we either must be on fire with His love, or be consumed by his wrath.

2. And at the same moment, there went out a fire from the Lord, and consumed them, and they died before the Lord.

A soul consecrated to its God, and which has devoted itself to Him; a soul who He has called to serve Him by pure sacrifice, can never admit any strange love, self-love, or self-interest, but it *dies* that very moment, and dies *by the fire coming forth from the Lord;* for the fire of His justice issues no less from Him than does that of His love. And this death is caused by its issuing out of its state, this infidelity being a death to the purity of the same state, which happens to it *in the presence of the Lord*, during its life even, ceasing as much to live in Him alone, as it desires to live by itself; and dying to the perfection of the divine life, just so much as it will not die to its own self-love.

> *6. Moses said unto Aaron, and unto Eleazar and Ithamar, his sons: Uncover not your heads, rend not your garments, lest ye die, and the wrath of the Lord be kindled against all the people. Let your brethren, the whole house of Israel, bewail the burning which the Lord hath kindled.*

He desires that amongst the priests and Levites, the most consecrated to the Lord, there shall be no mourning for the loss of these persons taken away by God: because he wishes the sanctified souls to enter into the interests of the Divine justice, without regarding any human interest. Did they commit this infidelity even under good pretexts, they would by that, issue out of their state, and would merit the same punishment. An inviolable faithfulness is needed, not to make a resumption in anything after having given one's self to God. The common souls may be afflicted at some loss, out of a feeling of compassion; and that passes with them for a good, and indeed can be so, when it is inspired by charity, or by a reasonable, though human, affection. But those before spoken of, must, in all things regard the sole interests of God alone.

> *7. But for you, go not forth from the door of the tabernacle; else ye shall perish: for the oil of the holy anointing has been poured upon you.*

He adds – If (by some turning back to your-selves, or for some particular interest) *ye only go out of the door of the tabernacle*, which is but for God alone, and in which ye ought always to stand enclosed; if ye stop at some voluntary reflection, *ye shall perish*, and issue out of your state; since having been consecrated to God by the *oil of the holy anointing,* which is the indelible mark of the character of a soul arrived in God, He is not willing that, by a single look, you should share in the grief and interests of the common souls.

> *44. I am the Lord, your God: be ye holy, for I am holy.*

The *holiness* that God demands of us, is a holiness relating to His own. Now, the holiness of God is in Himself, of Himself, and for Himself; it is therefore necessary that the holiness of these souls be in God, of God, and for God. It must be in God, existing only in Him, otherwise it would be proprietary, and would rob Him of something; and of God, seeing that all holiness that is not received from God, cannot be called such; and must serve His glory. The soul then arrived into God has no longer anything in itself, for itself, nor of itself; but by its loss into God, everything in itself, any more than it comes from itself. But, as everything has come from God, so has everything flowed there again. This then is the holiness proper to this degree.

> *45. For I am the Lord, that have brought you out of Egypt to be your God: Be ye holy, for I am holy.*

This verse is the confirmation of the preceding one, and further explains it. God declares that He *has brought* this people out of the land of their captivity, which was their own inventions, so as to lose them into Himself. This expression, *that I may be your God*, means, that I may be all in all to you Myself, in Myself, and for Myself. He no longer says, that I may be in you, or the midst of you: for this would be too little; nor that I may be for you; but, that I may be your God. Not for you, but in Me, and for Me. *Be ye then holy, for I am holy.* Be holy with this holiness, for it is Mine.

46. This is the law of every living animal.

47. That ye may know to discern between the pure and impure.

Ye *shall discern by this law of all that liveth* that which is perfect or imperfect; and ye shall also know by it, that the *love* that I exact of you is alone *pure* and upright. It is not that, for souls living in themselves, there is not a law less perfect, which they can and ought to follow, not knowing any other; but for the souls living in God, they must make this difference; because, that which is good for others, would be *impure* for them; and it is given them to know with more light, what they ought to embrace or reject. But the others have not yet the perfect disinterestedness [discernment].

Chapter XIV.

14. And the priest shall take some of the blood of the trespass offering, and shall put it upon the top of the right ear of him who is to be purified, and upon the thumb of his right hand, and upon the great toe of his right foot.

This manner of *purification* denotes that the soul that is clean and pure enough to enter into the most advanced way of the spirit, must have *the ear* consecrated to God alone, in order to listen to Him: for here it no longer uses words with God, at least ordinarily, unless He lead it Himself to say something to Him, which very rarely happens. For this reason, the ear is purified, and not the tongue; that may be silent before God, and be faithful to hear Him. *The thumb of the right hand is purified* moreover, which signifies that all the actions of this soul must be consecrated to God, and be done all in the uprightness of His spirit – God being Master and Author of them, as well as of the affections, denoted by *the feet,* which must be wholly pure, and of holy steps. But the right foot only is consecrated because the soul must carry all its affections to God, without ever turning aside or doing anything for itself out of an interested motive. Therefore David made this prayer: "Conduct me, Lord, in Thy way, and make me to walk in Thy truth." He meant in God Himself: for God is truth as well as charity, from which we ought never to turn aside.

CHAPTER XV.

   This whole chapter contains but an *exterior* and legal *purification*, an attention to which would appear unworthy of God, did it not signify His intention to instruct a gross and carnal people, and exhibit also His purity; of this He desired to impart to them a high idea (suited to their state), by this exterior purification, which was that of clothes so often purified and washed, and which, not being able to bestow purity upon the soul, was but an outward sign of what God exacted of this same soul. For God, having established this law of outward purification, on account of the grossness of this people, shows in the Gospel what a little thing it is – reproaching the Pharisees with being contented to cleanse the outside of the cup, whilst within it is full of extortion. The Christians of the present day do the same thing; they are contented with cleansing the outside, with affecting an apparently regulated life; although within, they are full of usurpations and plunder of God: for, if robbing men is accounted so criminal, how much more so is it to rob God? Jesus Christ then has taken care to instruct us how much these exterior purifications, bearing only the figure of the interior, were of little value and account, compared with this interior purification, which consists in taking away all rapines from within, restoring to God the usurpations and thefts that we have committed. He shows us the way, by poverty of spirit, renouncing ourselves, bearing our cross, and following Jesus Christ.

I believe, then, that all the fruit that we can draw from this chapter is, to make apparent to us the purity that God exacts of those who are His, as much inwardly as outwardly, which is but a very gross figure; that we are no longer washed in *water,* but in the blood of Jesus Christ, in which we can plunge without ceasing. This is what we ought to do the very instant we perceive ourselves to have committed some fault, by accident, or even willingly, to make a simple and sincere return to Jesus Christ, more or less active (according to the soul's degree), as its prayer is more or less active, or by a simple return – a plunging into God – into this sea of love – which will purify us from all our filthiness, much more than all the water in the world.

The offerings after the purifications were *pigeons* or *turtle doves* – showing that the most agreeable sacrifice to God is that of simplicity. A simple soul is immediately re-established in the grace of God, and in His pure love, and as promptly as a straw is consumed in a great fire, provided it does not issue out of its simplicity.

There are two kinds of oblations: the first is simply *offered* to God, and well represents the purification made by simple returns to God after faults of inadvertence or pure weakness. The sacrifice of *burnt offering* which was made of the other turtle dove, admirably signifies the purification of a more advanced state, wrought by holy love, in which the soul always remains like a burnt offering, not only to be purified, but to be consumed in this same love, in which it seems to change form and nature – to have no other form than that of this divine fire – and this is the thorough and radical purification which can only be wrought by pure love.

CHAPTER XVI.

1. The Lord spoke unto Moses after the death of the two sons of Aaron, when they offered a strange fire before the Lord, and were killed.

Nothing is of greater consequence to a soul drawn to God, than not *to offer strange fire*. Its fire must be pure, clean, upright, inviolably holy for God; without which, it merits *death*.

There are two kinds of strange fire; the one more gross, the other more subtle and dangerous. The first is the attachment to some created thing out of ourselves; riches, honor, fortune, persons, etc.; in fact, all that is not God Himself. The second strange fire is self-love and propriety, which are enrooted and identified is us; it is offering a strange fire to burn our incense upon this profane fire. The *incense* denotes prayer, as the Apocalypse declares it when it says that the four and twenty elders held each a censer before the throne of God, which were the prayers of the saints. Prayer, in order to be perfect, must be produced by pure love, which melts and dissolves, so to speak, the soul, as the gum of the incense is melted and dissolved in the fire, so that this soul, melted thus (if I may speak so) by the loss of propriety, which kept it fixed in itself, hindering it from flowing and losing itself in God, and, being perfectly disappropriated by pure love (which alone can do it), is lost absolutely to itself, flowing into God its last end.

> *2. And the Lord said unto Moses, Speak unto Aaron, thy brother, that he enter not at all times into the sanctuary within the vail before the mercy-seat which covers the ark, lest he die; for I shall appear in the cloud upon the oracle.*

How comes it that God does not desire the high priest *to enter at all times* into the Tabernacle? It was that at that time God might be more reverenced by the people, who, having only low and gross ideas of Him, were also conducted only by terror or extraordinary things – miracles and prodigies. Since the birth of Jesus Christ, this so great and holy God has rendered Himself familiar to men; but alas, how much they have abused Him! Terror is perhaps more advantageous to them than this immensity of goodness. It is thus with evil hearts; but, for good hearts, how much more are they touched by His love, than by all imaginable miracles! But how rare are these good hearts!

It is also to be remarked that God said *He would appear in the cloud upon the oracle.* This is an admirable faith that the soul truly has a perpetual access into its center, where God dwells. God covers and envelops, so to speak, His majesty with a cloud; everything is done and accomplished in this divine obscurity, in which the soul neither sees, feels, knows, nor discerns anything but a profound silence; but it is certain through faith that this is God; it cannot doubt of it; since He has chosen, as He has said in another place, the darkness for His hiding place. This adorable majesty, enveloped for the soul with clouds, has something infinitely more august and certain, than all that is discovered by the senses and faculties – as relishes, visions, revelations, ecstasies, and the rest – which are received either in the senses (and these are the more gross) or in the faculties, which are less so, but which are always of very little account compared with these sacred darknesses, which in this life serve for the communication of very God, as the light of glory serves in the other.

3. And let him not enter therein until he has offered a calf for a sin offering, and a ram for a burnt offering.

It was necessary that the high priest should be entirely purified before entering into the Tabernacle, according to all the purification of the ancient law, which was done by the shedding of the blood of animals – a more extended purification than that of water, since it not only served (like water) for legal purifications, but also for sins; although this blood had no merit in itself; but all its value was included in that which Jesus Christ was to shed. It was necessary then, that the high priest should be purified by the blood before entering the Tabernacle which was covered with a cloud. Likewise, the soul must also be purified from all its filthiness, in the blood of Jesus Christ, after having been so by the waters of the tears of repentance, in order to be admitted into this cloudy center, where God dwells. What purification must it not bear! It is only Jesus Christ who can purify the soul to the necessary point. Not only must it be sprinkled with His blood, but wholly washed in it. Adorable Savior, nothing is done but by Thee; and although Thou art them objectively concealed from the soul, it discovers afterwards, when it is more advanced, that it is Jesus Christ who has performed all these things, "Everything has been made by Him; and without Him has there been nothing made." It is then Jesus Christ who prepares and purifies the soul, until He has rendered it pure enough for it to be lost into God, and hidden there with Him.

After the high priest had offered up the *calf for the sin offering,* the *ram* must be offered *as a burnt offering.* This marks the last purification, which can only be made by this pure and divine love consuming everything, and destroying it so absolutely, that nothing remains. This is why pure love is truly the sacrifice of burnt offering, in which all propriety is destroyed.

> *4. He shall put on a tunic of linen; and shall have linen breeches, and shall gird himself with a girdle of linen; and with a linen mitre shall he be attired; for these garments are holy; and he shall put them on after having washed in water.*

The *linen* garments with which the high priest was to be clad, very well designate a pure life – simple and innocent outwardly – observing all the rules of outward decency and modesty, so as to edify and not to scandalize the neighbor – concealing the inner, covering it with this veil of simplicity and innocence. Nothing is commoner than linen; nothing is more common than the life of these souls who are simple and innocent, childlike and little.

> *7. He shall present two goats before the Lord at the door of the tabernacle of the testimony.*
>
> *8. And he shall cast lots upon the two goats; the one lot for the Lord, and the other lot for the scape-goat.*
>
> *9. And he shall offer a sin offering of the goat on which the Lord's lot fell.*
>
> *10. But the goat on which the lot fell for the scape-goat, he shall present living before the Lord, to offer prayers upon him, and to send him away into the desert.*

These two goats represent that innocent Lamb who has been willing to be offered up for our sins, that admirable *scape-goat*, charged with the sins of His people.

We can also see here a soul purified up to the point, called lost with Jesus Christ in God, who is then placed in the Apostolic state, to aid his brethren; but, moreover, who, like *the scape-goat*, is laden in some manner with their iniquities. After being charged with the curse of those for whom he suffers, he is driven *into the desert.*

There are two kinds of deserts. The first relates to ourselves, and through which we must pass before being able to aid others – the desert of ourselves – this separation and division from all things and ourselves, by dying to and renouncing everything – by quitting ourselves, so absolutely that we no more take part in what regards us, than if we existed no longer – leaving ourselves destitute in God's hands, and lost in Him for time and eternity.

The other desert is that to which the Apostolic man is often banished for his brother's sake. He must bear his weaknesses, be exiled, so to speak, from God, on account of him, bear his different dispositions, be driven into the desert; for he has been made a scapegoat for his brethren; and this is an extension of the mission of Jesus Christ, and of the Apostolic life.

The lots cast upon the two goats, and the destination made of them by the Lord, marks that all purified souls are not called to the Apostolic life. There are some admirable souls, of whom one has no knowledge, who are sanctified in secret, and who will be known only in the other life; these are the saints *consecrated to the Lord*, as this goat is consecrated.

These two goats also represent two kinds of persons, called of God to be offered up to Him by different sacrifices. Some by the loss of themselves unto God, peculiarly belong to Him, and He destines them to the most eminent grace, which is, to be reserved for Him alone, and to be sacrificed to Him without reserve and without there remaining to them any means of preservation. Others are destined for good works – for the service of the people and divine gifts; and the latter save their souls.

This lot clearly enough expresses the singular and efficacious calling of God, for one or other of these two ways. Those destined for holy activities finish their life thus and holily, meriting great crowns before God, as the price of their labors and services they have rendered to souls. But for those who in this life are destined for God Himself, Oh, what their life must cost them, and how mercilessly they must be *sacrificed!* Each one must be faithful to his way, respecting that of the others; and without judging or despising them, we must consider that every one has received his proper gift of God, and that what puts a value upon the states, is the will of God, by which we are there, and the faithfulness with which we remain therein: as it is also what constitutes all our perfection.

> *12. And he shall take a censer full of burning coals of fire from off the altar, and his hands full of sweet incense beaten small, and he shall enter within the veil in the holy of holies.*
>
> *13. And he shall cast the incense upon the fire, so that the smoke thereof may cover the oracle that is upon the testimony, and he die not.*

This is another sacrifice here, which is made only in the holy of holies; because it is altogether interior and the soul must have almost attained to its end before it is offered. It is *the sacrifice of the incense* dissolved by the holy *fire* of love, in which prayer is but *a smoke of incense*, in which the soul as it were liquefied in the divine love, does nothing but flow into God, where the sweet smell and smoke of the whole interior unceasingly ascends up unto Him without ever returning below, and where the soul having the honor and glory of God alone in view, with no more self-interest whatever, mounts unceasingly on high. And this sacrifice is of a sweet savor, ascending to the throne of God, who accepts it willingly. This is the sacrifice of thanksgiving of which David speaks, Psalm cxvi. 17, in which the soul has eyes only for God: it would have Him loved and glorified, it knows that He alone merits everything, and it returns all to Him. It is also the sacrifice of entire disappropriation: there remains nothing of the dissolved incense but a faint pleasant odor after the whole cloud has ascended. I believe that this is in the most perfect sense what St. Paul calls the sweet savour of Jesus Christ (2 Cor. ii 15).

It was moreover necessary, that the *smoke should cover the whole oracle*, that the high priest might not die. In this state, everything is hidden by the obscurity of this fragrant cloud, so that the soul might neither see nor discern anything in God, (all being covered with darkness, and faith being the real light of this life); and might no longer see itself; for to look upon ourselves brings death, as also does curiosity for things God does not Himself discover to us.

*16. And let him purify the sanctuary of the un-
cleanness of the children of Israel, the transgressions they have committed against the law, and of
all their sins. He shall do the same thing for the
tabernacle of the testimony, that has been raised
amongst them, in the midst of the uncleanness they
have committed in their tents.*

It seems that the sins of the people sully the
Lord's *sanctuary.* This is so true, that the destruction
of the Temple was only caused by the sins of the Jews,
as they were threatened: "I will profane my sanctuary,
I will destroy it and the Sabbaths," etc. (Ezek. xxiv. 21.
– Lev. xxvi. 31). It was necessary then to *purify the
sanctuary from the sins* of the people. But this was
not enough: it was needful to purify their habitation
and the sanctuary that was *in the midst of them,* without which their sins would have always sullied this sanctuary. It is just the same at the present time. The Church
in itself is all pure and spotless as was the Tabernacle;
but we pollute it by our crimes. How will it be purified
from our filthiness if we are not converted? If we do
not purify ourselves, we are by our sins the cause of
all the misfortunes that unceasingly happen to it. It is
in vain that we say, we wish to reform the Church. Let
us all turn ourselves to the Lord; let us reform ourselves, and it will be reformed. It is without spot or
wrinkle: it is we who cover it with mud and shame. O
Lord, do Thou reform our hearts! This is the only reform needed.

17. And when the high priest shall enter into the holy of holies to pray for himself, for his house, and for the whole assembly of Israel, there shall be no man in the tabernacle until he come out.

When God ordains *that there shall be no man in the tabernacle when the high priest enters into the holy of holies,* it denotes to us, that when God enters our sanctuary, which is the center of our soul, we must keep the soul entirely void of all gross and earthly objects, and still more of self; no distraction must enter into this sanctuary, no attachment, nothing, nothing to which the heart may incline.

There are some good souls, who, hearing this, may be troubled at having distractions in spite of themselves, certain vague thoughts which they cannot prevent. Let them not be disquieted; for all these do not enter into the sanctuary; they are only in the court of the temple. God permits these things to deprive us of the knowledge of what passes within the holy of holies, just as He concealed from the eyes of the people what took place in the sanctuary. When the heart is empty and detached from everything, distractions can do no harm: but those that proceed from attachments must be corrected by cutting away all kinds of ties and affections through a total death to all things.

21. And Aaron shall lay both his hands upon the head of the goat, and shall confess all the iniquities of the children of Israel, all their transgressions, and all their sins, putting them upon the head of the goat, and shall send him away by the hand of a fit man into the wilderness.

The high priest laid both his hands upon this scape-goat, upon whose head he confessed the sins of the whole people. I seem to see the Eternal Father applying His justice to Jesus Christ, as this priest laid his hands upon the goat: for it is certain that Jesus Christ has felt all the weight of the hands of a God, which is the weight of justice. Job, the most patient of men, desires his friends to have pity on him, for the hand of God had touched him. If this simple touch was so grievous, what must the weight of this mighty hand be!

The confession of sins represents the Eternal Father in applying His justice upon His son, ladening him with the innumerable multitude of our crimes, the deformity of which He showed to him: Therefore, the Prophet says, "He was laden with our iniquities, and by his stripes we are healed." *They loaded this goat with the curse.* Has this Divine Savior not been made a curse for His people, as it is written; "He has been made a curse for us," and again, "cursed is every one that hangeth upon a tree." Has He not been driven from amongst the men He came to save? Has He not been in the desert with no other company than the beasts? This was then the figure of Jesus Christ laden with the sins of all men.

29. And this shall be a statute forever unto you: that on the tenth day of the seventh month, ye shall afflict your souls; ye shall do no work with your hands, whether it be one born in your own country, or a stranger that sojourneth among you.

30. For on that day shall be made your expiation, and the purification from all your sins: ye shall be purified before the Lord.

31. For it is the Sabbath of rest, and ye shall afflict you souls by a perpetual worship.

At this time *ye shall afflict your souls*. This might be taken for a figure of active repentance, were it not added, *ye shall do no work with your hands.* There are two kinds of active repentance: the first consists in afflicting simply the flesh by fasts, penances, austerities, mortifications, so as to reduce this flesh to subjection; the second consists in having, as Scripture says, a broken and contrite heart, and the regret of having offended so good a God, who merits all our love and gratitude, but which we have only paid with ingratitude.

There is also another repentance which may properly be called passive, in which our soul is afflicted by the privations of perceptible consolations and supports. We afflict our soul to excess, by our reflections upon the graces we think we have lost, because we do not feel, nor even perceive them any longer. It is at this time *that we must do no work with our hands,* and wait in repose until the Lord manifests Himself. It is then that the soul passes beyond all the purifications before spoken of, expressed by *every work,* and from which it must cease: for nature always ardent, seeking out supports, and desiring consolations and something to satisfy it, places itself in a hundred postures to recover what it thinks it has lost: - it only causes itself to be dried up the more.

It is then of great consequence at this time, not to act by ourselves, and to passively suffer ourselves to be consumed by pain, that it may have all its effect, and purify us according to God's design. Our activity prevents justice from acting: it is only an entire rest that gives it room to act: thus Scripture assures us, that after these times of purification, we *shall be purified before God* of all our sins, which can only be by entire disappropriation. There is a great difference between appearing pure before men, and being really so before God. Simple, active purification makes us appear pure in the eyes of men; and truly so; but we are very far from being such in the eyes of God. Passive purification, or entire disappropriation can alone do that.

It is added, *for it is the Sabbath of the Lord, and ye shall afflict your souls by a perpetual worship*. It is after being purified before God that the soul enters into this so memorable a Sabbath, which is not our Sabbath or rest, but the Sabbath of the Lord, in which the soul passing into God finds in Him this perfect *rest and perpetual worship;* since it is wholly employed for Him, and by Him, not being able to be moved by any other thing. This worship is made in God Himself for Himself. Might I dare to say that it is the worship of God in God, and not in us? This supreme adoration is as much exalted as the creature ennobled and elevated to God through the loss of itself can render it.

But it will be said to me, if the soul is in this perfect repose, with what can it be *afflicted*? With nothing that regards it. It is this perpetual worship that afflicts it, for it knows what God merits, and the little it renders to Him. It is either God who in this perpetual worship inflicts suffering upon it, either to render it more conform to Jesus Christ, or for others; or it proceeds from so many creatures, to whom it must respond and correspond on account of its pilgrim state. This affliction may indeed invest the soul, but cannot penetrate to the center – this divine sanctuary which God has chosen for His Sabbath or place of repose.

> *32. This expiation shall be made by the high priest, who shall have been anointed; whose hands shall have been consecrated to perform the offices of the priesthood in his father's stead; and he shall put on the linen robe, and the holy garments.*

Who is he *that must make this expiation?* It is this High Priest, this admirable Priest after the order of Melchisedec. It is to Him that it is given to do it, and none can do it but He; it is He who has been *consecrated by anointing* in the midst of His brethren, and more than them all; for having been made man, He has become our brother: it is He who was sanctified by anointing, that He might sanctify the others, *and who performs the office* of High Priest *in His Fathers stead* for the expiation. This has an admirable sense. God the Father owed to His justice the punishment of the guilty: it was necessary, in the nature of things, that our crimes should be punished to satisfy His justice which would lose nothing of its rights. But this well beloved Son, this admirable Priest has received the anointing for the expiation: He has received upon himself the bolts of His justice, and has shown mercy on men; He has obtained for them a grace of mercy which would have been useless a attribute in God, were there not some wretched ones on whom to exercise it. Justice has had in Jesus Christ and though Jesus Christ a satisfaction infinitely greater than it could have taken in the punishment of all men. Thus this admirable Priest having made satisfaction, justice has given place to mercy to be shed on men.

Jesus Christ in becoming man *has put on the linen robe and the holy garments*. He has purified the Tabernacle and the people, changing a figurative worship into a most holy one; He has sanctified the people not by blood of victims, but by His own blood.

CHAPTER XVII.

3. What man so ever there be in the house of Is-
rael, that killeth an ox, or lamb, or goat, in the
camp, or out of the camp,

4. And bringeth it not to the door of the taber-
nacle to be offered unto the Lord; he shall be guilty
of murder; and he shall be cut off from among his
people, as if he had shed blood.

5. Therefore the children of Israel shall bring unto
the priest the victims they have killed in the fields,
that they may be offered unto the Lord, before the
door of the tabernacle of the testimony, and that
the priests may sacrifice them unto the Lord, as
peace offerings.

Why does God exact so rigorously *that all*
beasts killed should be offered to Him, who declares,
that these kinds of victims and burnt offerings are not
agreeable to Him? For they had truly no value, but what
they borrowed from the future sacrifice of Jesus Christ;
their value lay not in themselves but in what they signified. God exacts this ceremony to instruct future

races in the obligation under which they are of rendering unto God through Jesus Christ what they have received from Him, teaching the Israelites from that time a certain disappropriation proportioned to the state in which they were. For we must not believe that God was otherwise glorified by this prodigious effusion of blood shed *at the door of the tabernacle,* but in so far as that represented this adorable blood which the Lamb without spot was to shed before His Father's eyes for the salvation of His people.

> *6. The priest shall sprinkle the blood upon the altar of the Lord at the door of the tabernacle of the testimony; and shall burn the fat for a sweet savour unto the Lord.*

> *7. And they shall no more offer their sacrifices to demons, to whom they abandoned themselves in their fornications. This law shall be eternal for them and for their posterity.*

When God desired *a burnt offering to be made of the fat of the victims*, it was to show that He wished the best things in man to be consumed by the holy fire of His love, to be to Him a burnt offering of a sweet savour. It is this Divine fire which consumes all propriety in good.

It is added: *that they may no longer dedicate themselves to demons. To sacrifice to the demon* is to sacrifice to self-love. All works that are not offered up by pure love to God's glory alone, and which look to other than Him, are consecrated to self-love. How

34

is it to be understood what God says, that those men who sacrifice it to the demon, or self-love, *give themselves up for fornication?* It is in the same sense as that which is written: "Thou shalt destroy these adulterous souls that have withdrawn themselves from thee," (Ps. ixxii, 27). God is the Creator of souls, their Savior, their Spouse: it is to be adulterous, and to commit fornication, to draw back from God in order to love something out of Him, or not relating to Him. This is why it is necessary for everything to be first of all *consecrated to God*, and afterwards distributed to the neighbor according to His will.

> *10. And whatsoever man there be of the house of Israel, or of the strangers that sojourn among you, that eateth any blood; I will set my face against him and will cut him off from the midst of his people.*

This prohibition to *eat blood* is to make us understand that we must not stop at everything carnal, sensible, or sensual; but allow the earth to resume all these things which pertain to it, so that the spirit pure and disengaged may draw near God, and be united to Him, who is the end of its creation.

CHAPTER XVIII.

2. Say unto the children of Israel: I am the Lord your God.

3. Ye shall not act after the customs of Egypt, wherein ye dwelt; nor after those of the land of Canaan, into which I shall bring you; and ye shall not walk after their laws and ordinances.

4. Ye shall do my judgment, ye shall observe my precepts, and shall walk according as I have commanded you. I am the Lord your God.

God begins this chapter by these words: *I am the Lord your God:* as if He said; it is I who have a right to command you as your Lord and God; hear My words, that ye may obey Me. I have a right to command you in every way; and ye could not withdraw from My obedience without rendering yourselves rebels worthy of death. I command you then as your Lord and God, *not to follow the customs of Egypt or of other peoples:* as if He said: Follow not the maxims of the world: for if ye are mine, ye must no longer belong to the world: quit the multiplicity of Egypt, to enter into the simplicity of My children: cleave only to Me: shun the world My enemy: I bid you follow Me and hear Me, I, who am your God and Lord alone: *ye must follow my ordinances,* lose all self-will in such a manner, that you have no longer any other will but Mine.

> *5. Keep my laws and my ordinances; and the man that keeps them will find life therein. I am the Lord.*

If ye always do My will, so that ye *keep what I ordain,* and lose all self-will into Mine: *then shall ye find life*. It is by the loss of our own will into God's that we find a true life: for Jesus Christ becomes our resurrection and our life. He who is not with God, dwells in death. Is it possible to live without Thee, oh true, and only life of the soul? Thou art our God, and an Almighty God, to give us a life infinitely more abundant than what we lose in Adam, when we are willing to die wholly to ourselves in order to live but in Thee and from Thee.

> *27. All those who have inhabited this land before you, have committed those abominations, by which it has been defiled.*

> *30. Keep my commandments. Commit not what has been done by those before you, and defile not yourselves by these abominations. I am the Lord, your God.*

All those who have been before you, have defiled this land by their execrable abominations. This is what may be said at the present time, that almost all follow after iniquity and lying, in withdrawing from God. Alas, how much I fear that it will happen to this perverse race to be punished when they least think it! Scourges overwhelm us everyday, and we pay no attention that it is for our iniquities. If we *imitate the crimes* of those God has punished so severely, why should we escape them, let us turn to the Lord our God with all our heart, with all our soul, and we shall find life: for *He is our God*, who will make us new creatures in Him.

> *2. Speak unto all the congregation of the children of Israel, and say unto them: Be ye holy, for I am holy, I, who am your Lord and God.*

God desires His people to be *holy, for He Himself is holy.* So soon as we cease to be holy, we degenerate from this quality of the people of God: and this God so pure and holy. But what holiness does God require of those who are His? Let us not conceive it to be a usurped holiness, to attribute to ourselves what we find only in God Himself. What God requires is an entire exterior and interior purity of heart and mind, so that we may be able to draw near to this so pure a God, whose holiness is so formidable for criminals, as has been mentioned above: for this same Scripture, or rather God Himself who says to us: *Be ye holy, for I am holy,* also says HOLINESS BELONGS TO HIM WHO IS. We must then leave Him His holiness without usurping it; but become sufficiently pure to approach Him, and lose ourselves in this abyss of holiness of God; not for ourselves, but in Him and for Him. Be holy, oh my God, and purify us in such a manner that we may not be opposed by our impurities to this infinite purity and holiness, which flows in little streams upon the blessed and upon the faithful people of the Lord.

3. Let every one reverence with fear his father and his mother. Keep my Sabbaths. I am the Lord your God.

God bids us *honor our father and mother*; for they fill His place upon earth, and He has made use of them to impart to us the life of the body – without which we should have been destitute of being, and of the happiness of knowing God. But how badly observed this commandment is! Children despise their fathers, weary of their existence, and kill them a thousand times with grief: the bad treatment that the greater part of fathers and mothers receive from their children, is incredible; nevertheless, it does not go unpunished in this life, for often the children find themselves dealt with as they treated their parents.

God also bids us *keep his Sabbath days*. These Sabbaths of the Lord are not a simple cessation from outward work, as some persuade themselves; but first cessation from all works of iniquity; then cessation from our own works, that God Himself may operate in us, in order to enter into this true Sabbath, which is the repose of the soul in prayer, and afterwards in God its latter end. This last is the eternal Sabbath, a lasting rest, commencing in this life to endure forever.

4. Turn ye not unto idols, nor make to yourselves molten gods; I am the Lord your God.

We turn unto idols when we depart from God in order to turn towards the creature, whatever it be. When we prefer the creature to God, we make an idol of this very creature. Is it not written that avarice is idolatry (Col. Iii. 5). We commit idolatry in every disorderly love. What idolaters there are amongst Christians!

5. If ye offer unto the Lord a peace offering, that he may be favorable unto you,

6. Ye shall eat it the same day, or the day after it is offered; and ye shall burn up with fire all that remains until the third day.

7. If any one eat of it two days after, he shall be profane and guilty of impiety.

When the soul has arrived at the central repose, it may then be said to *offer to the Lord a peace offering*: for it is as a victim offered to its God in a passive state, to suffer everything, interiorly and exteriorly; inwardly, all crosses, afflictions, persecutions; in general, all that happens to us from God, from men, from demons, from ourselves by our imprudence's and faults.

How comes it that the peace offering must be *eaten on the same day it was offered, or on the morrow?* It is to teach us that the soul abandoned and at rest in God, is content with the divine moment, without preparing anything for the future. Its sustenance is the present moment of God's order over us. *The re-*

41

mains must be burned and *consumed by the fire*. What are the remains? After giving oneself up to the divine moment, and preparing nothing for the future, there come turnings and reflections, which must be allowed to fall, and be wholly consumed in this fire of divine charity.

If one ate of this peace offering several days afterwards, he was guilty of impiety. This marks how much foresight for the future is contrary of *abandon*; and how there is a time for profiting by the present light, after which we can no longer succeed in it. This is what Jesus Christ taught: "Profit by the light while it is day." The present moment must then be the life of the peaceful soul.

> *9. And when ye reap the harvest of your lands, thou shall not wholly reap the corners of thy field, neither shalt thou gather the ears that remain.*

> *10. Thou shalt not glean thy vineyard, neither shalt thou gather the grapes that remain; but thou shalt leave them to be taken by the poor and the strangers. I am the Lord your God.*

God gave this commandment to the Jews, to turn them from all avarice, and to induce them to *leave to the poor*, a part of what the Lord had given them.

> *11. Ye shall not steal. Ye shall not lie one to another. And, let no one deceive his neighbor.*

God absolutely forbids *theft*; so that, by learning to preserve equity towards men, and not usurping what belongs to them, we may at the same time learn this equity towards God – robbing Him of nothing, and usurping not His rights. This is why it is also written: *Ye shall not lie one to another.* For he who reckons himself something, whilst he is nothing, is a liar. He who wishes to be esteemed of men, *is a deceiver.* Of all knaves, thieves, and liars, there are none more criminal than the hypocrite; he robs God of His glory; he imposes incessantly on men, desiring to appear what he is not; he deceives himself; he is full of rapine, and of all iniquity.

> *12. Ye shall not swear falsely in my name: and ye shall not profane the name of your God. I am the Lord.*

There are many people *who swear falsely* – promising God on oath no longer to offend Him, and turning back to it without ceasing; others who use the oath to deceive their brother, profaning God's name to employ it in fraud – these people are condemned already. Hypocrites swear falsely: they have always God's name upon the mouth, to deceive and impose on men, and thus they profane His name, employing it in fraud and deceit.

> *13. Thou shalt not slander thy neighbor, nor shalt thou oppress him by violence. The wages of him that is hired shall not abide with thee until the morning.*

Calumny is indeed in use in this age. Hypocrites make use of it, thinking to raise themselves up on the ruins of their brother: party people likewise, believing that everything is permitted them, provided they succeed in their designs. Both make use of authority to oppress those they have calumniated; and this is the height of impiety.

The commandment *not to retain the wage of the hired servant* is a thing to which few people pay attention: by delaying payment, they cause both the workmen and their families to suffer; they oblige them to borrow, and thus ruin them. But if it is so great an evil to delay the workman's wage, how much greater a sin is it to retain his wage from him so that he loses it? There are some who give alms out of the food of others, causing poor artisans to suffer loss in order that they may perform almsgiving in an ostentatious manner. All that is an abomination before God. God desires equity in all things.

> *15. Ye shall do nothing against equity, and ye shall not judge unjustly. Thou shalt not respect the person of the poor, nor honor the person of the mighty; but in justice shalt thou judge thy neighbor.*

There is almost no longer any *justice* upon the earth. Judges are either partial, having a party in view they are so strongly prejudiced, that injustice appears to them justice; others allow themselves to be corrupted. It is very rare that a poor man with a good cause can gain it over a rich man whose cause is bad. Would people solicit the judges were it not to instruct them in the state of matters? There are everywhere honest people, and the world is not absolutely destitute of equitable judges, but how rare they are! And how many there are who oppress the innocent, when *authority* gets mixed with it.

> *16. Thou shalt not be amongst thy people an in-ventor of crimes, nor a secret slanderer; neither shalt thou plot against the blood of thy neighbor. I am the Lord.*

There are two kinds of persons *who invent crimes*: those who, committing new crimes, boast of those they have not committed; and others, who invent crimes against their brethren to torment and persecute them, taking away their reputation from them; these are the *secret* and hidden *slanderers*, a thousand times worse than those that slander openly, to which one gives but slight, credence; but these secret slanderers give weight to their slander and calumny, and thus render it without remedy. These libel makers who make no dif-ficulty in inventing and publishing the greatest falsi-ties, depriving honest people of their character, and rendering the calumny immortal by their writings. Oh, how severely will those persons be punished!

> *17. Thou shalt not hate thy brother in thine heart: but thou shalt rebuke him publicly, lest thou sin in not correcting him.*

> *18. Thou shalt not seek to avenge thyself, nor bear any grudge against the children of thy people; but thou shalt love thy neighbor as thyself. I am the Lord*

Brotherly correction is a delicate thing, and seldom used. Some correct their brethren publicly, not because they have erred, but because they hate them: others cry out against them, making known to all, crimes that they invent themselves. In order to correct our brother, we must be without passion, and have the right to do so. If we have no authority to correct him, he must be left in God's hands, without decrying him.

We are forbidden to *avenge ourselves.* Who is there who does not avenge himself with all his might, and who does not say that there is nothing more sweet than revenge? To hear and *forget injuries*, are commandments of both Testaments. Who is there that practices them?

This whole chapter is full of nothing else but precepts of equity, that God desires us to keep. It is only to be remarked, that in all the commandments that God gives in this chapter, He adds almost after every verse, *I am the Lord,* for two reasons; first to awaken the attention of this people, and to keep them in awe; secondly, to mark that He wished to be obeyed, and that He had the right to exact a blind obedience from these nations. For what God desires the most from us is entire obedience, and death to our self-will: and we may believe that when He gives so many ordinances to this people, and these of so little things that it appears even unworthy of this so Great God, to command in detail things apparently so childish, it is to teach them, and us, this blind and unreasoning obedience. It is sufficient that He who is OUR LORD AND OUR GOD command us to do anything, for us to do it, without regard to the importance of the commandment. For obedience in little things is more perfect than in great things, which bring their dignity with them. Moreover, little occasions are frequent and daily, and do not allow the suppleness of the soul to fall asleep.

The diversity of these commandments, their frequency, their littleness, render, by degrees, the soul supple and docile. Although we are no longer under the law of rigour, God does not the less exact from us our obedience. Men at the present time have but ten commandments, which they violate without ceasing; and the Jews were exact in this multitude of commandments. It is true that they feared punishment, and had not this obedience of love that God exacts of His children.

Chapter XX.

7. Sanctify yourselves, and be ye holy: for I am the Lord your God.

8. Keep my precepts and observe them: I am the Lord that sanctifies you.

God again repeats to the soul that He desires it to be *holy:* to make it understand that it must always advance in purity: which is done in proportion as it issues out of itself to be lost into Him.

But He assures it at the same time, that it is He who sanctifies it; so that it may learn no longer to seek holiness in the creature, nor perfect purity in any created medium; since it is in God alone that it can be found.

26. Ye shall be holy unto me; for I am holy, I, who am the Lord, and have severed you from all other peoples, that ye should be mine.

He adds, that not only will he sanctify them to

render them *holy* like the others; but that they will be holy for Himself, and not for them, having separated them for Himself from all other peoples of the land. All other men may aspire to holiness for themselves; but these here are chosen to be holy for God. Thus are they holy with the holiness put on in God and for Himself.

CHAPTER XXI.

8. Let them be holy; for I myself am holy, I, who am the Lord that sanctifies them.

This commandment of God so often times repeated, well shows that this people must not think they can be sanctified of themselves, nor be content with a middling holiness. He Himself, desires to sanctify them, that they may possess holiness in all its breadth, which is the holiness of God; since He sanctifies them by His own holiness.

CHAPTER XXV.

*55. The children of Israel are my slaves, since it is
I who have brought them out of Egypt.*

Oh happy captivity that of souls abandoned to
God! They are never freer than when they are more in
bondage. To be *God's slave*, is to be so dependant upon
Him by the gift we have made to Him of our freedom,
that we can no longer use this free-will, except by submission to His divine movements. God commands as
a sovereign, and the soul no longer resists Him: it indeed feels itself a slave; but it is so sweet a slavery,
that it would not be otherwise, preferring it to all the
liberty in the world: and the more its captivity increases,
the more also does its freedom increase, as the creature can never be more truly free than when it is wholly
swallowed up in the will of its Creator.

CHAPTER XXVI.

3. If ye walk according to my precepts, and keep my commandments, and do them,

6. I will establish peace in your countries, ye shall sleep in repose, and none shall make you afraid.

By this universal *peace* which God promises to *establish* on behalf of those that keep His commandments, may be well understood the general peace of the passions and faculties, with which He gratifies whose who give themselves up perfectly to Him. For some time they labor in the active way, and endeavor to obtain for themselves the peace of the passions by the religious observance of the commandments of God; but without being able to succeed therein, Nevertheless, in consideration of their labor and pious pursuits, God, by placing them in the prayer of quietude of His infinite goodness, gives them not only the peace of some passions, but peace in them all, and adds also thereto the peace of the faculties, which *sleep* with so gentle a slumber, and so strong as a whole that can *make them afraid*: all the creatures' threats, and everything that can be said against these souls, alleging that they destroy themselves by this way, and that they are idle in it, can no more turn them from it, nor make them change their resolution.

> *11. I will set my tabernacle in the midst of you, and my soul shall not reject you.*

This quietude of the whole soul is the disposition for the first union, by which God comes to dwell by a particular presence in the midst of the tabernacle. He, indeed, *sets his tabernacle in the midst of it*; but it is not yet made the Tabernacle itself; for then the union is not immediate, and there are yet means of union, and the tabernacle is a means and partition; for in the matter of union, every means forms a partition, being placed between the two things it united in order to join them.

> *12. I will walk among you; and I will be your God, and ye shall be my people.*

God, however, promises this soul not to reject it. He is so good, that He never rejects us, unless we quit Him ourselves first by our infidelities. He *walks* with the soul; and it always with Him: He declares Himself peculiarly its God and protector, and it is an admirable commerce of love.

> *15. But if ye break my covenant,*

> *16. I will punish you soon by poverty, and by a heat that will dry up your eyes and consume your souls.*

17. I will look upon you in anger, ye shall fall be-
fore your enemies, and ye shall be subject unto
them that hate you. Ye shall flee when none
pursueth you.

The soul has no sooner withdrawn itself from
the submission it owes to its God, than it falls into a
thousand evils. It retires from *abandon* to God, who,
fighting for it, rendered it victorious over its enemies,
in order to return to its own efforts, where it finds but
weakness and falls. It is even so greatly enfeebled by
its own strength in which it trust, that, without fighting, it falls at the very sight of its enemies; it is so
filled and troubled with panics after its infidelity, that
it *flees when none pursues it,* removing itself so much
the more from simplicity and union with its God, the
more it advances in its practices, and buries itself in
its own efforts. *The drying of the eyes* stands here for
the annihilation of the Divine lights, which are destroyed
by an imaginary fire and *ardour* we procure for ourselves; and then the soul is consumed, for we sow for
nought, and labor much without fruit.

18. And if ye will not yet for all this hearken unto
me, then I will punish you seven times more for
your sins.

God speaks now to his abandoned ones, who
truly do not return to their own practices; but who also
do not hearken to Him to quit themselves in the things
He desires, and allow themselves to be conducted as it
pleases Him, by the impenetrable paths of his wisdom,
fearing to abandon themselves too much to God. Then

he makes them suffer *seven times more for their sins*, causing them to undergo weaknesses and trials which he would not cause the greatest sinners to suffer: for the punishment or entire purification of sinners, is reserved for the other life: but for these chosen souls, God draws them out of their proprieties by hammer blows, and by the excess of suffering; and thus such extreme interior pains, as are described in the spiritual life, come only from propriety; and they are marvelously well depicted in many parts of Scripture.

Oh that I could explain here what it is *to be punished seven times more*, and how much God causes a light infidelity to be paid with usury, by the appearance of sin and pain of sin and often by sin itself; and how propriety, pride, and self-subsistence are something so insupportable before God, that it usually happens that He permits falls to beat down pride, or at least an appearance of fall, this secret being reserved for His judgment alone! Is it not as St. Paul expresses it? "Lest," said he, "I should be exalted by the greatness of my revelations, a thorn in the flesh, a messenger of Satan, has been sent to buffet me"; as if he said; lest I should appropriate to myself the graces of God, an experience of the lowest misery teaches me what I am by myself, and keeps me in an entire destruction in the midst of the greatest Divine gifts.

> 19. *I will break the hardness of your pride. I will cause the heaven to be over you like iron, and the earth like brass.*

The first *hardness of pride* here *broken*, is the self-support the soul had in its gifts, graces, and its own strength. The second, is this *hardness* in it caused by propriety, previously mentioned, which places a real impediment to Divine union. To destroy this pride and propriety, God shuts *heaven* for this soul: it is *rendered like iron* to it: there no longer flows from it a pleasant dew; God has nothing now for the soul but apparent rigours: He seems no more to listen to it, but rather to reject it. It no longer finds any consolation in heaven or earth: for the earth has become *like brass* to it, in which it can no more taste its sweetnesses. Then this soul finds itself in inexplicable anguish, of which experience alone can give a conception.

But I assure those persons who are in these pains, that they come only from their proprieties; and that what they believe to be great trials from God, are proprietary pains that they know not of: let them, however, abandon themselves, quit all resistance, giving themselves up fearlessly and unreservedly into God's hands, not by formal and distinct *abandon*, which still imparts some support; but really, leaving themselves without hesitation to God's will, allowing themselves, moreover, to be stripped of all good without stirring or resisting, bearing all the enemy's attacks with supreme immobility, without even fearing; being assured that God can alone overturn all our enemies. But so soon as we enter on the defense of ourselves, that is sufficient to cause our fall at their approach alone.

23. But if even after these things ye will not be reformed, and will continue to walk against me;

24. Then will I also walk contrary unto you, and will strike you seven times for your sins.

God continues to assure these souls that *if* they *still walk* in their first *resistance*, not suffering themselves to be conducted by Himself where He desires, He will increase their punishment in this case: He will not be content with not listening to them, and being stern towards them, so that the heaven remains inexorable, and the dew no longer flows upon them; but He Himself will moreover be *opposed* to them. Oh, if it was known what it is to have God against us, and what frightful torment we suffer thereby, alas, to what would we not abandon ourselves sooner than see ourselves reduced to this extremity? Job, feeling the weight of his horrible destitution, piteously complained that God having become *adverse* to Him, he was a burden to himself. But the creature is so proprietary, that it prefers to suffer such strange things, rather than allow itself to be stripped of a virtue to which it is attached: it thinks even to gain merit by suffering so many ills in order to retain it: but it greatly deceives itself; seeing that it loses the real virtue by wishing to preserve its appearance: in place of allowing this appearance of virtue to be lost when it would preserve the reality.

These reiterated blows, with which God strikes this soul, because of its resistance, are weaknesses relating to mortal sins, with which He overwhelms it in order to make it despair of its own strength, and it lead it to abandon itself fully unto Him. The soul seems to itself to be nothing but pride. All its thoughts, words, and actions, are full of it: it feels more than ever attached to the earth and clings to it: it believes itself full of impurity from the head to the feet: it is tormented with jealousy and envy against the persons who belong to God with more *abandon:* it loses all mortification, and it seems to itself to be wholly sensual: it can no more rule itself in anything, nor be content; and the more it tries to do it, the less it succeeds in it: hatreds in the imagination, which it cannot conquer, render it desolate; often they would even seem to be directed against God: anger, which seemed dead for so long a time, wakes up; and hastiness rises up every moment.

All spiritual persons who do not abandon themselves, travel this road, more or less, according to the degree of their propriety, and God's design in their purification: and the more a soul has been elevated by the affluence of Divine gifts, the more profound is its fall by the experience of like distresses. I say, that all those destined for the mystic death go this way, (with the exception of some privileged persons, like the holy Virgin, who never having had the life of the criminal Adam, has not experienced the death of Adam): and it is because whatever fidelity they desire to have, they resist without thinking of it, even placing (for they are not enlightened) their fidelity in their resistance, and being astonished at their sluggishness and carelessness for all good, scarcely being able to perform it any longer; and bringing as much cold into holy things, as they formerly had of ardour in practicing them.

25. I will bring upon you the avenging sword of my covenant:and when ye would flee for refuge into your cities, I will send the pestilence amongst you, and ye shall be delivered into the hands of your enemies.

This *avenging sword of the covenant* is a knife of division which God brings to the soul, so as to separate the two parts, the superior and inferior, without which it would always resist. Oh, it is then that this separation causes the soul to suffer a strange agony! Seeing itself thus pressed, *it flees for refuge into the cities,* that is to say, it seeks some support in exterior actions, in the practice of virtues, in the conversation of the servants of God, in the frequenting of sacraments; but these no longer relieve it, for the grace of this degree is a grace of *death,* and it is to increase their loss; so that it sees itself, although for its greatest good, *delivered into the hands of its enemies.*

26.When I have broken the strength of your bread, ye shall eat, and shall not be satisfied.

God *breaks the strength of our bread,* when, instead of finding consolation in the holy communion, we find there nothing but disgust and new pains. It is a great trial for a good soul that has had respect and devotion for this Divine sacrament, to feel that it is no longer satisfied with this heavenly manna; but on the contrary is always more empty.

27. And if ye will not for all this hearken unto me, but walk contrary unto me,

28. Then I will walk contrary unto you also in fury; and I will chastise you with seven wounds for your sins.

When God sees that this soul, which He desires absolutely for Himself, *yet resists* His voice, He is not content with *walking contrary to it;* but He still augments its pain, and walks against it in *His fury.* Alas! Then it knows not where to turn: for God breaks it in His fury, as Job had experienced it (Job xvi. 10), his pains becoming extreme beyond all that can be expressed. Nevertheless, certain it is that it is only our resistance that causes them, at least, usually; although it is true that God sometimes inflicts them by His power, causing the purest souls to suffer interior griefs, thus Jesus and Mary suffered them, and St. Paul was often consumed by a sorrow and sadness of heart which his zeal for God's glory, and the salvation of His brethren caused him to suffer; but these sorts of pains are so pure and peaceful, that they may be called all-divine. The other pains caused by propriety, are generally accompanied by some trouble and inquietude, being, as it were, a devouring fire, which, by vigorous and profound operation, causes us to feel the rust and impurity that remain to be consumed. It was in this light that the prophet-king prayed God, not to "rebuke him in His anger, nor chastise him in His hot displeasure," (Psalm vi. i).

Now, the more resistance continues, the more are the pains redoubled; and it is then that God increases the affliction: for the second time there were but exterior blows for sins according to their distinction; but now *there are seven wounds for sins:* what before was superficial, appears here to have won completely to the interior, and to have formed deep wounds. Oh, what a great difference there is between blows and wounds, and how those who have experienced it know it well! They are the same trials in appearance, being made always upon the seven articles of the capital sins before mentioned; but how very different in their penetration.

> *31. Then will I make your cities waste, and bring your sanctuaries unto desolation, and I will no longer smell the savor of your sweet odors.*

God goes still further. He brings everything into disorder in this soul. *Its cities,* which are its exterior and interior senses and faculties, are brought into such a desolation, that they *are changed into wastes.* It is necessary, also, that the center, and most profound part of the soul, *the sanctuary,* be destroyed and annihilated: there no longer remains any image of holiness; and this God who dwelt there inhabits it no more. Ah! Then it is that this so holy sanctuary (but which nevertheless served as a medium between God and the soul), is destroyed with nothing remaining of it. Oh what a strange blow does the soul suffer by the loss of this sanctuary! It is nevertheless a good thing for it in its affliction, and a means of correction, too rude in appearance, but in reality too blissful. From that time, there is now no resource for it. Oh who can comprehend it! Nevertheless it is this total destruction of the Divine sanctuary, or the center of the soul, which soon ends all the trials.

34.Then shall the earth enjoy the days of her repose, as long as it lieth desolate.

As soon as the soul begins to *take pleasure* in its distresses, and desolation, and *in the repose* of its uselessness, and nothingness, delighted to be thus in its proper place, and to serve the glory of God by the loss of all self-interest; it is then usually that all its pains cease, and it is well nigh its end. But it is then also that it can cry, that it has been humbled even to excess, and finds its repose in the most extreme bitterness.

42. And I will remember the covenant which I have made with Abraham, Isaac, and Jacob.

45.And I will remember the covenant of their ancestors, whom I brought forth out of the land of Egypt in the sight of the heathen, that I might be their God.

Then God *remembers* that it is for Himself that He has brought His dear interior ones out of the country of multiplicity, and that they have been destroyed and annihilated by so many purifications and trials. Oh, then, He draws them out of this state of distress; for He is now *their God;* and no longer resisting Him it is for this alone that He has *brought them out of Egypt.*

Book II

NUMBERS

WITH REFLECTIONS REGARDING
THE DEEPER CHRISTIAN LIFE.

CHAPTER IX.

18. The children of Israel journeyed according to the commandment of the Lord, and encamped when he commanded them.

It is the property of a fully abandoned soul, to suffer itself to be conducted to God in such a manner, that it takes not the least step except by the movement of His spirit, ready to perform everything, or to quit everything (all being alike to it) according as it feels itself moved of God. And this is all that is needful for it.

21. If the cloud abode from the even till the morning upon the tabernacle, and was taken up at break of day, then the Israelites journeyed: and if it was taken up after a day and a night, they journeyed immediately.

22. Or whether it tarried upon the tabernacle either two days, or a month, or still longer, the children of Israel remained camped in the same place; and when it was taken up they journeyed.

These faithful abandoned ones regarded not whether it was *day* or *night*; whether they were in light or darkness: they had no set times or measures to take by themselves: but they left themselves to be conducted without hesitation or doubt, *journeying or staying* at God's pleasure with an admirable promptitude, troubling themselves neither about their advancement nor repose, everything being equal to them in God's will).

Chapter XI.

1.There arose nevertheless a murmuring amongst the people from those that complained of their labor against the Lord. And the Lord heard it, and his anger was kindled: and the fire of the Lord burnt amongst them; and consumed the uttermost part of the camp.

It is so strange a thing this nakedness and desert of faith, deprived of all support, that the soul has great difficulty in remaining contented and faithful therein, without repenting of having bound itself to a way so long and so hard for the senses. For although God is its conductor, yet it has nothing to lean upon, for everything is obscure for it. The excess of this pain causes us *to murmur as if we complained* of God. But this is only followed by a greater affliction; for the soul enters into an interior *burning* so strange, that it suffers the pains of death: and this burning *consumes a part of the camp* which is the repose of this soul: but it is only the *uttermost part*; for this is the repose it took in itself or in the gifts of God, which must be taken away from it, so that it may unalterably rest in God and His will alone.

2. Moses prayed unto the Lord, and the fire was quenched.

Moses' prayer, or the simple return of the soul into its abandon, appeases the wrath of God.

4. A band of people who had come up with them out of Egypt, fell a lusting after flesh; and sitting down, they wept, and having also attracted the children of Israel, they said, who shall give us flesh to eat?

This other *people that had joined the children of Israel,* represent the feeble souls, and also the inferior part, which, being afflicted at this nakedness, desires something to feed upon. This feeble part *weeps* in a strange manner, seeing itself deprived of its food which it *lusts after.* It dare not, however, ask directly for what it craves; only it says, *who will give me flesh to eat?* Who will give me some consolation as food? It often even draws *with it* the superior part, which takes part in its pain, and thus sins.

6. Our souls are dried up: our eyes look upon nothing but this manna.

These unfaithful persons regret their past practices, nourishing their self-love. They pass in detail what they tasted in Egypt (which is a multiplied country) although these were things pitifully low and carnal. If God desires them to advance further, and that the superior part should have little or no share in these complaints, He gives them nothing; so that no sensible relief may hinder them from going beyond everything to press forward to Him alone. But when the will is mixed therewith, He gives them a delicious food that can content them. And these souls, not seeing that it is a punishment for their fault, believe they have obtained a great grace, in which they are much deceived.

People that are still self-interested say that God performs miracles on their behalf, and that He grants them what they ask: beyond that, they add, *our souls are quite dried up*, and there is nothing to sustain us: *We have nothing before our eyes but manna*, being in the obscurity of faith, which suffers us neither to see nor taste anything; so that we see only this same faith which wearies us: for the manna that is given us, although a pure and substantial bread, satisfies neither the taste nor the sight.

10. The murmuring of the people appeared unbearable to Moses.

The enlightened director has the greatest difficulty in bearing with the wanderings of these souls, who regret *the onions,* to wit, their low productions, and cannot be contented with so pure a food as that of faith and abandonment to God: this *appears* to him *unbearable.*

11. And he said unto the Lord; Wherefore hast thou laid on me the burden of this great people?

He complains lovingly to God of the yoke He has imposed upon him, *charging him with the conducting* of so many carnal souls, who have so much difficulty in following the ways of the spirit.

12. Have I conceived all this great people, or have I begotten them, that thou should'st say unto me; Carry them in thy bosom as the nurse carries the little child.

God's goodness is admirable in thus charging certain persons with so great a multitude of spiritual children, who must be carried in the bosom, nourished, brought up, and introduced into the promised land. Oh Lord, how happy are those to whom thou givest a Moses to conduct them. But this Moses has much to suffer. Alas! He is not only charged with instructing and aiding them; but he must moreover bear all their pains.

14. I am not able to bear all this people alone, because they are too heavy for me.

15. If it please thee, I pray thee kill me if I have found favor in thy sight, that I may no longer be distressed by so many afflictions.

He suffers the pains of death seeing their infidelities: not, however, pains of regret or of trouble, but pains inflicted by the hand of God: so that when proprietary persons approach such as Moses, they cause them to suffer the pains of hell; and it happens but too frequently, that seeing themselves charged with a great people, who through infidelity do not render themselves pliable to grace, they *long for death* or deliverance from these afflictions.

God often releases them in part, associating with them persons who may aid them to bear the yoke; thus He gives here *seventy elders of Israel* (v. 16) unto Moses, to aid him in conducting His people.

> *18. Thus shalt thou say unto the people: sanctify yourselves: tomorrow ye shall eat flesh.*
>
> *19. Not for a day only, nor two days, nor five, nor ten, nor even twenty days.*
>
> *20. But for a whole month, until it come out at your nostrils, and it be loathsome unto you.*

God gives this people what they desire, and contents their taste by some sensible gift for some days, and sometimes even for a long time. This causes them to believe that they have accomplished everything, and have entered on a new life, although it is but a state of pure sensuality and self-love. *When* the Lord says to them, *sanctify yourselves and ye shall eat flesh,* it is as if He said: since ye will not have the Lord to sanctify you, sanctify yourselves; return to your practices, and ye shall eat flesh, that is to say, ye shall taste the pleasures of the senses that you esteem spiritual; (which is only to satisfy the gluttony of the spirit:) eat of them until ye be so filled that you are *disgusted* with them, and recognize the value of the former food.

> *21. And Moses said, there are six hundred thousand footmen in this people, and thou sayest, I will give them flesh to eat for a whole month.*

Moses still doubts after so many assurances of the Divine power: but this is only done for our instruction. God permits such doubts in His servants, that out of them may come the oracles He Himself pronounces in replying to them. Such was that of the Apostles on the subject of the multiplying of the loaves. *There are here,* said they, five barley loaves and two fishes; but what is that among so many? But Jesus took occasion thereby to instruct them, and to perform His miracle.

> *23. The Lord answered him: Is the Lord's hand waxed short? Thou shalt see now whether my word shall come to pass unto thee or not.*

But God shows how everything is easy *to the might of His arm,* and that nothing surpasses His power since it is infinite; we do Him wrong when we measure His power by our feeble reason. Thus does He assure us, that *His word,* which appears often so incredible in the mouth of His servants, *will be verified by His works,* and that one day the effects of His power will be seen in the very things that were thought the most impossible.

> *25. The Lord took of the spirit that was in Moses, and gave it unto the seventy elders, and they proph esied.*

Whoever is established in God alone, is so bare and disappropriated of all good, that he suffers everything that had been given him to be *retaken* without resistance, being delighted that it should be *imparted* unto others, for he seeks not his own glory, but the glory of God only.

> *28. Joshua said unto Moses: My lord, forbid them to prophesy.*

> *29. Moses answered him; Why art thou jealous for my sake? Would God that all the people prophesied, and that the Lord would put his spirit upon them.*

This extremely pure zeal for the glory of God alone causes *Moses* to give such a beautiful *reply to Joshua.* Persons well annihilated do the same when souls of grace are concerned about their glory; they do not mind if they lose everything for the interests of God and of souls. *Why,* say they, *is any one jealous for us?* We must be jealous only of the jealousy of God. Who is jealous but of His own glory. Thus we ought to be jealous only for God's glory. We should, like Moses, ardently desire *that all* had attained to the same state, and *had* the same *spirit of God.* Oh how beautiful are these words of Moses, and how they ought to be livingly imprinted upon the hearts of all those who serve souls by the ministry of the word of God and sacraments! *Would to God that every one prophesied, and that the Lord would put his spirit upon them!* St. Paul had the same feeling when he said: "What then? So that in every way Jesus Christ is preached; and I therein do rejoice, yea, and will rejoice." All true lovers of Jesus Christ ought to be like so many faithful echoes of this voice, which emanates from a disinterested love.

33.The flesh was yet between their teeth, and this food was not consumed, when the anger of the Lord was kindled against this people, and he smote them with a very great plague.

Oh poor souls, tasting new delights which ye thought to be great graces, and which, nevertheless, were but the object of your spiritual concupiscence, God makes you purchase this little pleasure very dearly. You are yet all full of these apparent sweetnesses, when He sends upon you out of His mercy and justice *a great* and frightful *plague.* If it was known with what a terrible plague of death God punishes the spiritual gluttony and sensuality of souls, who, after having tasted the manna of pure faith, return to the sensible, people would be terrified. Ah how much better it is to suffer the first severity of mercy in destitution than to experience that of justice in a favor procured by sensuality of the spirit.

34. This place was called sepulchers of concupiscence. And having come out of the sepulchres of concupiscence, they came to Hazeroth, where they abode.

As God has only merciful justice for us, even in His greatest severities, this so strange a punishment in these persons is generally the *sepulchre of concupiscence;* for it is by this long and terrible punishment that they lose all carnal desires in the things of God; and that, leaving in this place all desires, *they come out thereof* without delay to dwell in another place more advanced.

CHAPTER XI

1. Miriam and Aaron murmured also against Moses.

2. And said, Hath the Lord only spoken by Moses? Hath he not also spoken to us? And the Lord heard it.

3. .Now Moses was very meek above all the men which were upon the face of the earth.

It is a common thing for passive souls, when they are in the peace of this state, to think they have passed through all the states; and as they have quite a natural desire of speaking and writing of the things of God, they persuade themselves that they are in the degree of consummation. But they are very far distant from it; and although they say that they have the same spirit as Moses (that is to say, as the souls arrived into God alone), and that God makes them hear the same *language,* they deceive themselves greatly.

God, seeing this mistake, Himself takes the part of these persons, so *holy* and so *consummated* in Him;

for they have then so great a *gentleness that there is nothing like it upon the earth;* because it is no longer the meekness of the earth, but the meekness of heaven and of God Himself. This *meekness* is not remarked here for nothing, since it is one of the principal qualities that distinguish the souls that are in God alone from the others.

> *5. The Lord having called Aaron and Miriam to the door of the tabernacle,*
>
> *6. Said to them, If there be among you a prophet of the Lord, I will make myself known to him in a vision, or I will speak to him in a dream.*
>
> *7. But* my *servant Moses is not so, who is the most faithful in all my house.*
>
> *8. For I speak with him mouth to mouth, and he sees the Lord clearly, and not by enigmas or figures.*

These words of God contain so clearly and literally the difference there is between these states of passivity and light, and that of God alone, that it is necessary but to repeat the same words in order to have a conception of it. God communicates Himself to the souls of light *by visions and dreams,* under shadows and *enigmas,* which form some division between Him and them; but for the deified souls, He *speaks* to them *mouth to mouth,* and, as it were, essence to essence, by infusion, and not otherwise. And it is this essential word that is infallible, and which can only be received into the essence of the soul, from whence it flows upon the faculties when it is to be expressed. This is what constitutes their difference from the first, whose grace being more in the faculties is thus sensible, distinct, and perceptible. God adds, that this soul in God manifestly sees the Lord, being placed in the truth of God Himself in God; but the others see it only obscurely and under shadowy images.

10. Miriam became leprous, white as snow.

This punishment of Miriam shows how God does not fail to smite these presumptuous souls with the leprosy of a thousand weaknesses, which covers them for seven days. This relates to the seven mortal sins, and (as has been previously mentioned, Lev. xxvi. 24) this is the usual punishment of these kinds of souls.

13. Moses cried to the Lord, saying, Oh God, I pray thee, heal her.

14. The Lord answered, Let her be shut out of the camp for seven days, after which let her be received again.

God grants Moses this cure of his sister only after she has passed seven days in a kind of banishment, that is to say, when she has suffered all the weaknesses that relate to the seven mortal sins, and has borne the confusion thereof before all the people. These souls in their weaknesses are known as such of every one; and this is what causes their real abjection, and is the sure antidote of their presumption.

CHAPTER XIII.

2. The Lord said unto Moses:

3. Send men that may search the land of Canaan, which I give to the children of Israel, one man out of each tribe, every one a ruler among them.

24. They cut down a branch with one cluster of grapes, and they bare it between two upon a staff.

The land is only known by its fruits. This prodigious *bunch of grapes,* carried by those who had been *sent to search the land,* is a proof of its fertility. *Now* this fruit is *a grape,* preserving in itself the delicious wine of pure love, not for itself, but for him who expresses it. God has all the glory of it, and the neighbor all the benefit. This *bunch of grapes* marks also the union that souls arrived into God, who is *the promised land,* have amongst themselves; thus the grapes are all united in the same bunch. But this union is founded upon Jesus Christ, who is the grape and *the vine.*

28. Surely it is a land flowing with milk and honey, as may be known by its fruits.

There flow from this *land,* which is God, our center, our origin, and end, rivers of *milk and honey.* The gentleness of the persons who have happily entered therein is without limit; and there flows from them an affluence of divine words wholly mild and agreeable, serving as milk and honey for the little ones.

31.Caleb said, Let us go up, and enter into possession of the land; for we are able to overcome it.

A soul full of confidence looks for everything from God's goodness and strength; therefore, filled with courage, he also animates the others. *Let us go,* says he, let us fear nothing, although amongst apparent difficulties; for *we can obtain* by God's goodness what we could not conquer by our own strength; and it is easy for Him to enable us to overcome, according to His promise; "in God shall we do great things, and He Himself shall tread down our enemies."

32. But the men that went up with him said: We are not able to go up against this people, for they are stronger than we.

On the contrary, souls full of trust in themselves, looking upon it only on the side of their human strength at first despair of ever being able to succeed and turn aside the others from it, saying that they are too weak to aspire to so elevated a state. It is true that *if* we take it in the light of our own strength, man can never attain it; but, on the part of *God,* everything is possible, and faith only is necessary for that, according to the promise of Jesus Christ: "If thou canst believe, all things are possible unto him that believeth."

CHAPTER XIV.

1.The people cried with a loud voice and wept all that night.

2. And all the children of Israel murmured against Moses and Aaron.

It is strange that they who are full of self-love and trust in their own strength should have so much power to weaken by their false reasoning's the faith and trust of abandoned souls, throwing them into such disorder that they even give way to tears and groans for having quitted their first captivity, in which they thought to live in safety, although with great pain. They blame their conductors; they accuse them of being the cause of this loss; and this is a common thing for all the feeble souls who speak to these persons full of self-love, who detail to them sad examples, in order to turn them from this pure way, and to assure them more strongly of their destruction: they spare nothing therein, not being able to suffer people to trust themselves fully to God.

3. Would to God we had died in Egypt! Would to God we had perished in the wilderness, that God had not brought us to this land, for us to fall by the sword, and our wives and children to be taken captive! Were it not better for us to return into Egypt.

It is a frequent thing for these persons to regret *not having died* in the land of multiplicity, in which they believed their salvation much more secured. They see, however, that there is no means of *returning into Egypt,* for all the passages are shut: They wish, at least, *to die in this great desert of faith,* in which there remains a little hope, not yet being altogether lost.

They well know that God alone can bring them into this land promised to them; therefore they say, *Let not the Lord conduct us there.* They enter into distrust of His goodness and power, and by their infidelity issue out of *abandon,* which causes them an incredible affliction. Oh poor blind ones! You think that so many enemies, whose strength is shown you in proportion as you recognize your own weakness, must be destroyed by your own strength! Ah, how you are deceived! This is why you say that *your wives and children—that* is, your inferior part and senses—are going to remain forever in a new *captivity,* and that you yourselves are going to *fall under the sword* of sin. No, no, you will never fall if you come not out of *abandon;* and the evil that you do yourselves by thus distrusting God is greater than all those you fear; for in souls of your degree, this is the source of all the sins you can fall into.

4. And they began to say one to another: Let us make a captain, and let us return into Egypt.

They are so blind that they still *consult* to *return* to their first activity without considering that this would be impossible for them; and that, no longer having God to conduct them, since He desires another thing of them, they would fall defenseless into the hands of other enemies more powerful than those they dread in the country that God desires to bring them into.

This *captain* is a new director they are desirous of choosing, that he may make them return to their former activities; a director who flatters their own judgment.

5. Then Moses and Aaron fell on their faces to the ground before the whole multitude of the children of Israel.

This *prostration of Moses and Aaron* denotes how easily very spiritual persons can give up the conducting of souls committed to their trust. Not so the others; they have a thousand attachments, and endeavor by every means to retain the souls under their direction. The former act in the manner they do, because they are annihilated; and, recognizing in themselves neither any goodness, nor strength to aid the souls that God gives them, they resign them without difficulty; but the others act quite the contrary by a strange presumption, believing themselves more fit to conduct than any other.

6. But Joshua and Caleb, who were of those who had spied the land, rent their clothes,

7. And said unto all the company of the children of Israel: The land which we have surveyed is a very good land.

8. If the Lord delight in us, then he will bring us into this land, and will give unto us land where flow milk and honey.

There are often found amongst the great number of these feeble souls persons both firm and advanced, who sustain the others, and who assure them from their experience of the *goodness* of this land promised to those who abandon themselves purely unto God, and the advantage of being established therein. They add, that it is easy to arrive there if *the Lord delight in them,* that is to say, if He conduct, and they suffer themselves to be conducted to Him, they will not fail to be brought into the land; for the reason why, out of so many persons who come out of the multiplied way, there are so few that arrive into God, and almost all die on the way, is this, that they enter into distrust, and thus slacken their pace and stop, and often issue completely out of the way.

9. Beware of rebelling against the Lord, neither fear ye the people of this land; for we can devour them like bread. Their defense is taken away from them, and the Lord is with us: fear them not.

Scripture declares that it is *rebellion* to issue out of *abandon,* and to be unwilling to be conducted to God, coming Out of His Divine order, and blind dependence upon Him, to enter by reflections on self-guidance; it counsels us that we must not *be afraid,* but courageously abandon ourselves; for with the strength of God *we can devour our* open *enemies,* and sin itself, *like bread,* without their being able to harm us; for they can only do so when we issue out of *abandon;* since while we remain in God's hands, all the power and malignity of sin is removed from us; and it, as well as all the demons, remains powerless against us, seeing that the *defense* and power of sin are its sting and malice; and these being taken from them, and God not withdrawing from us, but our will remaining united to His own, there is nothing to fear for us. But it must be remarked that I say so long as we remain united to God's will and in *abandon,* for out of that everything may harm us; nevertheless, we shall never perish except by distrust and want of faith and courage to abandon ourselves amidst all perils, without in the least regarding our own interest, or what may happen there from.

> *10. But all the congregation cried out against them, and desired to stone them. And the glory of the Lord appeared above the tabernacle unto all the children of Israel.*

Those under the influence of reflection, and alarmed from their fear, listen not to the wise remonstrance's made to them: they even *wish to stone* those that give them so good advice; that is, to wish to convince themselves by reasoning's proceeding from the hardness of their heart; but God, whose goodness is infinite, seeing them ready to perish altogether, sends them a ray of His light, which is *the glory* of His majesty quickly discovered to them.

> *11. The Lord said unto Moses: How long will this people murmur against me? How long will it be before they believe me, after all the miracles I have done before them?*

At the same time He justly complains of the *little faith of this people* who doubt, and thus would sink into the abyss, did God not stretch out the hand to them; for nothing wounds His goodness so much as distrust, above all, after having given us so *many proofs of his power* and protection.

> *12. I will smite them with the pestilence, and will consume them; but for thee. I will make thee the head of a great people mightier than they.*

> *13. Moses said unto the Lord: The Egyptians, out of the midst of whom thou hast brought this people,*

> *14. And the inhabitants of this land, learning that thou, who dwelt in the midst of this people, and were seen face to face,*

> *15. Hast killed this innumerable people as one man, will say:*

> *16. Because thou hast not been able to bring this people into the land which thou didst promise them, therefore thou hast slain them in the desert.*

God threatens to *destroy* these souls because of their incredulity; but no sooner are they interceded for than He pardons them. Now what is this prayer that His faithful minister offers to Him on their behalf? It is by representing to Him, that it is for His own glory not to suffer them to perish by abandoning them in their wanderings, from which they would all fall, destroyed by real sin (and not apparent) thinking to avoid a peril only imaginary, and falling really into a veritable abyss.

The annihilated man has no more self-interest; therefore, he does not even reply to the kindness that God shows for his person; but being concerned only for the interest of the way of which he has been constituted the guide, represents to God how active persons, seeing those who walk in the way of faith and simplicity fall by some visible disaster, may take occasion thereby to do two things, both unjust to God and to those who abandon themselves to Him.

First, to lay the blame on *abandon* in place of regarding the fault of the creature, which has only fallen from having issued out of *abandon.* They exclaim immediately: Behold what it is to abandon oneself! This way is nothing but deceit; far from having the power of conducting the soul to God, it only *draws* it from the care of itself (which is Egypt), *to bring it to perish in the wilderness* of faith, where, finding itself powerless, having lost the practices that sustained it, it *cannot* be *brought* to God as it hoped, since, on the contrary, He leaves it to perish as a punishment for its

93

rashness. Behold one of the common mistakes in the reasoning's of multiplied persons.

The other is, that they always endeavor to persuade people, that those who have unhappily fallen were the furthest advanced, and in the divine state of life in God alone, in which everything is in substantial union, and from which the creature cannot fall away except by a strange infidelity. Therefore they cry out, that they who have thus fallen were of the number of those to whom God *shows himself face to face,* as Moses remarks in this very place; which is an artifice of the devil to hinder souls from abandoning themselves; because this holy abandon takes away from him all power over them.

> *17. And now I beseech thee oh Lord, let the greatness of thy power shine forth, as thou hast sworn, saying:*
>
> *18. The Lord is long-suffering, and of great mercy, blotting out iniquity and crimes, and never abandoning the innocent.*
>
> *19. Pardon, I beseech thee, oh Lord, out of the greatness of thy mercy, the sin of this people.*

Moses then prays God for His own glory to draw these souls out of the extreme peril to which they are reduced, so that the others may not have the advantage of thereby taking occasion to condemn this way. He also brings before Him *his mercies*, and how He can as easily *blot out* this sin by His goodness, as He can punish it by His justice. He *beseeches* Him to pardon it.

> *20. The Lord said unto him: I have pardoned them according to thy prayer.*

> *21. I swear by myself, that all the earth shall be filled with the glory of the Lord.*

God pardons; but, in doing so, He declares that it is solely for the interest of His own glory that He grants this pardon, so that throughout the whole earth the immensity of His power to happily conduct souls that are abandoned to Him may be known. He swears by himself and His own life; to show by that life He lives in this way, and that it is by it He communicates His life forever.

> *22. But all those men who have seen my glory, and the miracles which I did in Egypt, and who have tempted me now these ten times, and have not hearkened unto my voice,*

> *23. Shall not see the land which I promised an oath unto their fathers; and none of those that have murmured against me shall see it.*

All persons who vacillate and hesitate so much, and who, issuing out of *abandon,* often enter into distrust; who, far from obeying blindly, *tempt God so many times* by their little faith; all these *shall not see the promised* land—that is to say, shall never enter into this life in God alone, but shall die in the desert and on the way. It is for this cause alone that they never arrive at it. Were they, instead, to allow themselves to be conducted by a blind *abandon,* without thinking of themselves, most assuredly they would arrive at the promised land. But, alas! Almost all die on the road; some sooner, others later; but all are deprived of the happiness of seeing it. Not only do they not enter, but they never have a true knowledge of it *by sight;* nor shall they who murmur against the way and decry faith and *abandon* to God, ever have the light of truth to perceive this way and land, that is to say, the repose of the soul in God; they shall never comprehend it in this world.

This figure expresses so clearly and fully the great number of those who through infidelity die on the road of the interior desert, and the small number of those who are faithful enough to arrive at the end, that scarcely in all Scripture will there be found another figure depicting it more naturally.

24. But my servant, Caleb, because he had another spirit within him, and hath followed me fully, him will I bring into the land which he hath spied, and his seed shall possess it for an heritage.

Caleb, being of a firm spirit and constant in faith, who had neither hesitated nor doubted, but had allowed himself to be conducted without resistance in blind *abandon,* who had already *seen the land,* and had already been there, coming out of the mystic state to enter into the divine, in which he is yet only on trial and not yet fixed for ever; this *Caleb,* I saw, so faithful, *will I bring into the land* which he has spied; I will give unto him this most permanent state in God alone, with which he is already acquainted, and into which he has entered transiently. *His posterity,* the souls of his stamp, who are not distrustful, and who without regarding themselves leave themselves in perfect *abandon, shall have this land for inheritance;* which means that they will possess it in a permanent and lasting manner, and that this state will become so intimate and common to them, and they will have advanced in it in such a manner that it will appear as it were natural to them; and they will dwell in it as in their inheritance.

Caleb was of the tribe of Judah, which represents the souls strong in Jesus Christ, who is the chief, middle, and end of this family; they possess the courage of the lion, for all their courage is in Jesus Christ, and they have no longer any of themselves. But of all the tribes, there is but that of Judah—that is to say, of all spiritual souls only those who, with a lion-like courage, abandon themselves to God's hands without ever drawing back, arrive into God alone. Nevertheless, this courage is not in them, but in Jesus Christ.

25. Seeing that the Amalekites and Canaanites are hid in the valley, get ye up tomorrow, and return into the wilderness by the way of the Red Sea.

Oh, if it was known what hurt is done to interior persons by doubts and distrusts, it would create surprise. These infidelities are the cause of much going back, therefore we see under the figures of this people who *turn back* when on the point of entering this so much desired country, souls retracing their steps and *returning* to the first desert from which they had set out. It is thus with many who pass all their life in doing and undoing, and who, without any notable advance, die at the end of twenty years in the same state, having done nothing but advance and go back; for we must necessarily do either the one or the other in the ways of the spirit.

26. And the Lord spoke unto Moses and Aaron, saying:

27. How long will this wicked people murmur against me? I have heard the murmurings of the children of Israel.

God calls those people *wicked* who speak against the way of truth by which He conducts these souls in blind *abandon;* and He is greatly offended at them. How could those be other than wicked, who are opposed to God and His dearest friends, and who fight against what He esteems the most? However good their intention may be, their zeal is not according to knowledge nor true discernment.

28. I swear by myself, saith the Lord, that I will do unto you *as ye have spoken in my presence.*

This *oath* that the Lord swears *by himself,* shows the magnitude of the offence which has been committed against Him. To doubt His power, is to doubt His Being; and it is to take away from His title of God either to doubt His power or goodness; His power to perform what He promises, His goodness to will it: thus He adds, *I will do unto you as ye have spoken in my presence:* as if He said, Ye shall be treated just as you have trusted yourselves to My power and goodness, and as ye have doubted both.

> *29. Your carcases shall fall in this wilderness, and all that were numbered of you, from twenty years old and upward, which hare murmured against me,*
>
> *30. Ye shall not enter into the land: Caleb and Joshua alone shall enter.*

Ye *shall all die* on the way and *in the wilderness,* without arriving at the end for which I had drawn you from your multiplied labors; *with the exception* of the children who like simple and young hearts, have not entered willingly into distrust, having only fallen therein out of pure weakness and by the influence of the others; or else, who maintaining their hearts in simplicity, although young and little advanced, have neither doubted nor *murmured.*

Out of six hundred thousand men and more who came forth out of the land of Egypt or multiplicity, *only two* arrived in God alone, all the rest having died on the road for want of faithfulness and *abandon.* This clearly shows that all are called to this way and end, namely, to return to their origin (which is God) if they were faithful enough to allow themselves to be conducted there. God calls them all, but very few attain to it. This, however, does not proceed from the part of God, whose goodness is infinite, and who fails not to offer the necessary means to those who are willing to make use of them. Not only does He wish all to be saved; but, moreover, that all should arrive at the end of their creation, which is God Himself; or rather, none can be saved, who arrive not at this end before entering into *the* enjoyment of salvation: which will necessarily be performed in the other life in each chosen one, if it has not been accomplished in this; for it is the Christian perfection, without which none shall enter into the possession of eternal salvation; nothing imperfect, nor the least *propriety,* being able to enter into God, nor into the paradise of His glory. Those then who do not arrive there, are deprived of it by reason of their want of faithfulness.

Those who find so much mention made here of faithfulness, will take this in an active manner, thinking that this faithfulness lies in taking precautions and observations, and in doing much on their own part. No, this is not the faithfulness of this degree, which consists only in believing and abandoning ourselves—in *believing* that God is all good, and all powerful; all good, never forsaking those that abandon themselves to Him, as He assures us by Isaiah; "Can a mother forget her child, and have not compassion on the son of her womb? Yea she may forget, but I will forget you never." If God then has so much goodness for all those that trust themselves to Him, to doubt it is to do Him the worst injury. He is equally *all powerful* to sustain us; "Thou shalt know," He says by the same prophet, "that it is I who am the Lord, and that all those who trust in me shall not be confounded," according as it is said of Daniel, that he received no hurt in the den of lions, for he believed in his God. The second point of this fidelity is *destitution*, never resuming ourselves through any cares of our own, never being anxious or concerned about our state, but remitting to God even our salvation, and our eternity. This is what is called blind *abandon*, looking to no self-interest, but suffering ourselves to be conducted to God, as a blind person is led by his guide.

> *31. And for your little children, whom ye said were to be the prey of the enemy, them will I bring in, and they shall see the land which has not pleased you.*

These *little children* are, as I said before, the simple and innocent souls, who, although not far advanced, yet arrive at the termination; for, without following their own reasonings, they suffer themselves to be conducted, like little children, without any concern as to where they are led. They do not sin, since they do not even know what sin is. These persons then, simple and innocent, *whom ye said were to become the prey of the enemy*, will be those that I Myself will lead into Me, and whom I shall cause to enter into the Divine life, in order that ye may know the advantage there is in trusting to Me, and the ineffable happiness ye have despised when I called you to bring you therein.

> *32. Your dead bodies shall be spread on the ground, in the desert.*

It is necessary that man be truly *dead* in order to arrive at the promised land, and not only that, but also that he should rot by the experience of his own abjection, according as Jesus Christ saith that "except the grain of wheat fall into the ground and die, it abideth alone." This rottenness then is the death of the grain, and death is the cause of its rottenness. And *these dead bodies* that rot *in the desert* are thus the figure of a frightful death and rottenness, which must be passed through interiorly in order to find a new life in God.

As for the unfaithful souls, God does not show them the promised land in this life, but *their bodies* being *dead,* they must remain *in the desert,* which is to perform their purification in the other world, and to serve as an example in this one, by the death which has surprised them before attaining to their perfection.

But the true mystic sense of this passage is, that God causes those who resist Him to pass through a death and abjection much more strange than the others who suffer themselves to be led without resistance; and, as they commit many infidelities, They remain in this state of death and rottenness with out ever coming out of it in this life. This is well expressed by the *dead bodies* that lie *spread on the ground, in the desert,* and it is as if God said to those that resisted Him, Ye shall be stretched by the sleep of death, in your own corruption, without ever coming out of it, whilst those whom I have withdrawn have happily issued from it, having believed and trusted in Me.

33. Your children shall wander for forty years in this wilderness, and they shall bear the penalty of your infidelities, until the dead bodies of their fathers are consumed in the desert.

The *children* are those who, through feebleness, have doubted, hesitated, and participated in the fault of the others. All must, without exception, remain for a long time in the way of faith, and not come out of this obscure *desert* of the mystic life, until all *rottenness is consumed,* for nothing of this rottenness can enter into God; it is indeed the road by which it is necessary to pass to arrive in Him, but nothing of it whatever can dwell there. It must then be wholly consumed *in the desert,* and be all reduced to ashes by total annihilation, which forms the end of every way, for it leads to the goal.

This rottenness is no other than the corruption proceeding from ourselves through the bad smell of the dead bodies of our fathers, that is to say, of the flesh, which has been corrupted by sin in Adam, for it is necessary, as says St. Paul, that "the body of sin be destroyed," and "we have the hope of being delivered from the bondage of corruption, to participate in the liberty of the children of God." And as all spiritual men have sinned, either by themselves, or in Adam, it is necessary also that all pass through the corruption and rottenness, caused either by their own sins, or by the dead bodies of their fathers. This is very evident.

34. According to the number of the forty days during which ye searched the land; a year will be reckoned for a day.

It is easy to see by this passage that, as has been said above, the observation of the land was nothing but the disposition towards the permanent state which it precedes, according to the usual conduct of God. Therefore it is said that *forty years will correspond to forty days,* and *that a year will be reckoned for a day.*

> *40. And they rose* up *early in the morning, and went up to the summit of the mountain, and said; We are ready to go to the place where the Lord hath commanded us, for we have sinned.*

Those who recognize that they *have sinned* through a resumption of themselves, commit a second fault as untoward as the first, it is that they wish to *ascend* to God again by their own efforts, and fancy they are able of themselves to arrive at their end: they strive then to *ascend even to the very top of the mountain.*

> *41. But Moses said to them, wherefore transgress ye the command of the Lord, since it cannot prosper?*

> *42. Beware of going up, for the Lord is not with you, lest ye fall before your enemies.*

But the enlightened director, seeing their error, warns them wisely *not to go up lest they fall before their enemies,* for those who place themselves in states of their own accord, perish there, God not being with them.

44. But they, being infatuated, went up even to the summit of the mountain. Nevertheless the ark of the covenant of the Lord and Moses departed not out of the camp.

45. And the Amalekites and Canaanites that dwell upon the mountain came upon them, and smiting them and hewing them in pieces they pursued them even to Hormah.

Those persons who desire to enter by their own efforts into the ways to which God does not call them, are so *blind* that in spite of advice they yet continue to introduce themselves therein. But neither God nor directors conducting them, they are *wounded by their enemies,* and are obliged to return with a thousand wounds.

Whence we ought to learn two great truths, first, that God alone can conduct souls in His ways; second, that we must not interfere therein, nor on the other hand excuse ourselves or hesitate when God calls us to them. Fear and rashness, distrust and presumption, are almost equally punished in this people. We must suffer ourselves to be conducted to God, following step by step His divine movements and obedience, without anticipating Him or drawing back, but by a total abandon leave ourselves as God desires, suffering patiently the retardment caused by the fall, drinking in with deep draughts the humiliations which it brings, and being well pleased that God should be satisfied throughout the whole extent of His justice without wishing to diminish any of it, content to remain all our life in our low degree, without aspiring or laboring to draw ourselves out of it unless God do it Himself, and then leave ourselves to be led as a child where He wills.

CHAPTER XV.

23. It shall be forgiven to all the people of the children of Israel, and to the strangers that dwell amongst them, seeing that this people have sinned through ignorance.

God shows here pretty clearly the difference that there is between interior persons who are His chosen *people,* and others who have not this advantage, namely, that the former commit sin only through *ignorance* and frailty, their will remaining united to God's, so much so that they would rather die than offend Him, and this is so true that when they think that what they have done is sin, they suffer thereby a mortal grief; moreover, did they sin deliberately, they would thus issue from their state, and from the conformity, union, or transformation of their will into God's, according to their degree.

God not being able to bear sin, should the will become guilty, that very moment it would necessarily be separated from God, which would place these souls in a hell, feeling assured of their sin being voluntarily committed. But so long as they remain in their *aban-*

don, in their resignation, in the union of their will to that of God, in a general sacrifice of themselves and of all that regards them to His good pleasure, generously preferring His glory to all self interest, in a lively experience of His pure love, and in an entire abandonment to His conduct, believe me, they have not sinned voluntarily although they may have fallen into appearances of sin, for all the fruits of grace, and of a preeminent grace, are incompatible with crime. Thus, although they assure you themselves that they have sinned, yet you will see that when in confession you ask them if they have a distinct knowledge of having sinned deliberately, they will, when pressed thus, say that they do not know of it. It is certain that grace exists in these souls, and that their will being retained in God, although under mystic darkness, is entirely separated from all that takes place in the inferior part.

29. There shall be but one law for all those who sin through ignorance, as much for the inhabitants of the country as for strangers.

This *law is also for the strangers* who have intercourse with the people, that is to say, for those who join themselves to the advanced spiritual ones, and who enter into the same state although they may not have been raised to it, and for all persons less advanced who sin unwittingly.

30. But whoever shall sin presumptuously, whether he be born in the place or be a stranger, he shall be cut off from his people, for he hath rebelled against the Lord.

Scripture confirms what has been said before, namely, that so soon as these souls sin presumptuously, as much the advanced ones, who from their birth have preserved the love of God, and who have entered early into this way, as well as those who, after growing old in other ways, have at last placed themselves in this one. So soon as they sin voluntarily, they must issue out of their state, and from being in conformity as before, they now become enemies, and thus are cut off from the people of God, being separated from those who are only that through the union of their will with God's This does not, however, hinder these sinners from repenting and being saved, but they no longer belong to this chosen people, who may indeed have wretchedness, and may commit faults through frailty, but who never can deliberately will to displease their Well-beloved, and consent to be His enemies, since by this they would issue out of the union with this so dear a people, whose proper quality is love.

It is then that there is verified what St. Paul says, that it is almost impossible for those who, having once tasted God and have since quitted Him, ever to return to Him, at least in a like degree to what they were before their fall. It is even more difficult for them to be converted than it is for great sinners, for no offence wounds the Well-beloved so much as to see a soul, on whom He has bestowed so many blessings, and to whom He has given to taste of the innocent pleasures of His love, voluntarily quit it, withdrawing from His arms where He held it embraced for so long a time, to delight in outward vanities and declare itself His enemy.

To think of this alone horrifies one, for then the will is a thousand times more wicked, and the spirit more perverse, than they ever were, having separated themselves from the Sovereign Good after knowing and tasting Him, which the others have not done. Thus there is more malignity in the disobedience of those who have had the more knowledge of God, and the more experience of His bounties; and the surest mark of their fall is, that they withdraw from their way to give themselves to outward pleasures, even decrying it, and publishing abroad that they have known its errors, and abandoning themselves in time wholly to sin; in place of which the others being united to God, and faithful to remain in His way, it must not be thought that they sin easily, although there may be seen in them the appearance of sin. And so long as they remain supple and obedient, abandoning themselves to God in spite of their miseries; so long as they are humbled by them, and desire not to offend God, although they may suffer extremely thinking they have sinned, yet, assuredly there is no crime.

CHAPTER XVI.

1. At that lime Korah, Dathan, Abiram, and On,

2. Rose up against Moses, and two hundred and fifty others with them, of the princes of the congregation and chiefs of council.

3. And gathering themselves together against Moses and Aaron, they said to them, Let it suffice you that all the congregation are holy, and the Lord is in them. Wherefore do ye lift yourselves above the people of the Lord?

It is a strange thing that the punishment they had just received upon the mountain for having desired of themselves to ascend higher than was permitted them, did not prevent them from following their presumption, and from wishing to encroach upon the charge of Moses and Aaron. It is common enough for the more advanced persons, before God calls them to this employment, to be desirous of mixing themselves with the conducting of others, fancying that they are better able to do that than those whom God has chosen for it. It is an error of the spiritual life, which slips into it even from its commencement, to be desirous of laboring for others unseasonably; and it is only a false fervour that leads us to undertake the aiding of them before we have received the talent and vocation to do so successfully. Many fancy themselves capable of conducting in the way of the holy who have scarcely entered therein themselves; and wishing to impart to others the graces that have been only given for them, they themselves lose the fruit, and cannot succour others with them. We must not set about helping the neighbor while we desire it, and have not the experience of divine things and the calling for it, for it is necessary first of all to be founded and established in the interior life.

Jesus Christ, our perfect model, passed thirty years in the hidden and unknown life (applying himself to continual prayer and remaining annihilated before his Father during a period so long that he might have been able to have done an infinity of good to the world), before employing himself visibly for the salvation of men; in order to teach us, by his example, to allow all eagerness to assist the neighbor to die out, and which is generally wholly natural, and to dwell in silence and repose until the time and moment has arrived when God will give us His word and command to labor for the salvation of souls, should He design to make use of us. As for Apostolic employments, I dare affirm that the permanent Apostolic life can only be given when the soul has arrived in God, and that in an eminent degree. This does not, however, prevent obedience from engaging therein, but when it is by obedience, God supplies what is wanting to the state, and He knows well how to do it, so that those who work according to His command produce all the fruit that he intends.

Some persons, even very spiritual, hearing me speak of the permanent Apostolic life, will take that for a certain ardour which passive souls have of assisting others; they possess within themselves so great a good that they would communicate it to all the earth. But these persons are infinitely far from the state of which I speak, which can never arrive until the soul be dead and resuscitated in God, and well advanced in God alone, where everything is found in divine unity. Then it enters into the Apostolic life permanently, by substantial effusion and by essential union, where it is God who acts and speaks in it without its anticipating or resisting Him, nor participating in any thing of its own in what is said or done by it, imitating thus the manner of speaking and acting of Jesus Christ, who said, I can do nothing of myself," and "I judge according as I hear," and also of the Holy Spirit of whom He says that "He will speak not of himself, but that he will speak all that he will hear." This must be understood thus.

The Persons of the Trinity as united in the Divine Essence are there all equally, and they speak and act by themselves as speaking and acting outwardly by one same essence in perfect unity, but as distinct Persons they receive each other, the Son the Father, and the Holy Spirit the Father and Son, by their eternal emanation.

Now I say that it is necessary for the soul to pass by Jesus Christ, and by the Trinity in distinction, before arriving in God alone, who is the essential and indivisible Trinity, everything being found re-united in the one Essence, in perfect unity, so that after having been united in Jesus Christ distinctly, and to the personal Trinity, according to the operations appropriate to the divine Persons, everything must be re-united in the point of Essential Unity, where all personal distinction is lost, and where we remain hid with Jesus Christ who is our life, in God, as St. Paul had experienced it.

The reason of this order observed in this reflowing is, that the soul having come out from the unity of the Divine Essence by the Trinity of Persons, and this Trinity having been communicated to it by the graces and merits of Jesus Christ, it is necessary also that in order to return fully to its origin, it should proceed by Jesus Christ, its mediator and chief, to the Trinity of Persons, and by it to the Unity of the Essence, where everything is reduced into perfect unity in the fullness of the divine life, and in unalterable repose.

But when the soul has become re-united in this essential point of God alone, it makes itself known outwardly by its deeds as the divine Persons by their operations; and thus it is multiplied in its actions, although it is perfectly one, simple, and indivisible by itself, so that it is one and multiplied, without, however, multiplicity preventing unity, or unity interrupting multiplicity. This must not be understood solely according to thought, sight, sentiment, conformity, or resemblance, known as such by the creature, but by a real and permanent state, although it usually is not known to the soul (that has the felicity of having attained to it), as in itself and for itself, but it is given to it to know it and express it as in others and for others.

In this state, however, it is not the creature which comes out to speak and act and produce the effects of the apostolic life. The soul has no part therein. It is dead and perfectly passive, or rather perfectly annihilated to every operation; but God, who is in it essentially in most perfect unity, where all the Trinity and personal distinction is found re-united, comes out Himself by His operations without ceasing to be everything within, and without quitting the unity of the center, He diffuses Himself over the faculties, performing by them and with them, sometimes the office of the Word, instructing, acting, conversing; sometimes the office of the Holy Spirit, sanctifying, setting on fire with love, melting the most secret places of hearts, and speaking by the mouth of this creature, which remains perfectly passive to all that God the Word, and God the Holy Spirit operate in it and out of it by its organism, whilst this soul (void of all propriety and distinction, not only of persons, but of itself), dwells essentially united to God in the center, which is God Himself, where everything is in the perfect repose of the essential unity of God, whilst also the same God acts by it in distinction of Persons. All this is wrought without the sight or knowledge of this creature, which is entirely incapable of making this discernment, and which knows its words and actions only when they appear, as it would those of another person. But God reveals this mystery to whom He pleaseth.

Now when the Word *(Verbe Paroles)* speaks by this soul, He can only speak by it what He spoke Himself whilst living upon the earth, so that this soul makes use of the words of Jesus Christ and of Scripture without seeking them or thinking that it does so. The reason is that Jesus Christ being Himself His word He can never speak but what He has spoken. And this speech multiplied outwardly is found re-united in the Word, and the Word in God, without personal distinction or multiplicity, but in the perfect unity of the essence, as St. John expresses it, "The word was in God, and the Word was God." *The Word was in God,* behold the personal distinction; *the Word* was God, behold the unity of the essence.

This is then what I call THE APOSTOLIC LIFE, namely, the state in which the soul being dead to everything, and perfectly annihilated, retaining nothing of itself, God alone dwells with it and in it, and it is sunk and lost in Him, living in its center only from its essential life, but issuing outwardly in its personal life, by distinction of deeds and not of knowledge. This is shown us in the great Apostles who were confirmed in the permanent state of life and apostolic employments only after the reception of the Holy Spirit with fullness, which caused in them an entire void of themselves, and so great a suppleness to all that God desired to operate by them that it is said "it was not they who spoke, but the Spirit of their Heavenly Father that spoke by their mouth, and St. Paul declares that it was Jesus Christ who spoke in him. Every one who is enlightened, or who has attained to this state, will understand me well.

I say moreover, that few persons attain to this state, and that very holy souls die in the consummation in God alone, without God having personally, and by effects, come forth in them. A particular calling is necessary for this, and when it arrives it in no way draws the soul out of its perfect unity in God alone: as neither Jesus Christ nor the Holy Spirit were drawn there from, although they act in a different manner outwardly: so that it is certain that on account of the essential and indivisible unity, when the Word acts outwardly, the Father and the Holy Spirit also act indivisibly with it, and when the Holy Spirit acts the Father and Son do so likewise, for they are indivisible in their operation with regard to the creature. This however does not prevent this perfect unity reduced into God alone, from changing names according to the multiplied effects proceeding there from, nor does it prevent as real a distinction of the Persons, as it is true that the Essence is one in itself, and according to the relation which the operations bear to the different properties of the Divine Persons, they are distributed amongst them differently: fertility and power to the Father, wisdom and providence to the Son, goodness and love to the Holy Spirit, and these are all united in God alone, where all is power, wisdom, and love.

These apostolic souls in whom this is wrought have neither movement nor tendency, however little, to assist and speak to the neighbor, but God furnishes them with everything by His Providence, and puts His words in their mouths as and when it pleaseth Him.

This being established, it is easy to see that there are very often some who commit faults similar to what is remarked in this part of Scripture, when, finding themselves in the passivity of light and love, they often take as from God what proceeds only from their own fervour, and there may be and there is often a deception. But in the state that I speak of here there is none, and can be none except by coming out of the state itself.

These persons say often, like *Korah:* We are as fit as the others to help the neighbor, since *all* that is in us is *holy;* but the sequel and experience will well show that though they be holy in themselves and for themselves, they are not yet holy enough to perform the office of priest and shepherd on behalf of others, this being reserved for those whom God has chosen for this employment.

It may also be known from this why so many workers, laboring much in the church of God, produce so little fruit. It is that they either meddle with it themselves without being called, or because they are not sufficiently established in Jesus Christ, nor united to Him in order to bring forth by Him great fruit.

4. And when Moses heard it he fell on his face to the ground.

Behold the true character of an apostolic man: not only does he never think of conducting any others than those whom God has entrusted to him, but besides he is ready at the slightest signal to quit everything, and far from disputing he gives way immediately, being ready never to mix himself in anything.

5. And he said to Korah and to the whole congregation, Tomorrow in the morning the Lord will make known those that are his, and will choose the holy ones for himself: and those that he will choose will come near to him.

This reply of Moses, and this manner of speaking, referring everything to what *God* will *make known* concerning it, is admirable. He says that God Himself will cause it to be known who are His, and who are these *saints* whom He has *chosen* for this ministry: but by what sign will they be distinguished?

6. Thus do ye: Let each of you take his censer, you Korah, and all your company.

7. And tomorrow put fire therein, and put incense thereon before the Lord, and whomsoever the Lord will choose he shall be recognized as holy. Ye are much lifted up ye sons of Levi.

One can scarcely distinguish these persons except by *fire* and by pure charity, which having God alone

119

for its object, as He is its end, sends up to Him an agreeable *perfume,* and mounts up straight to Him without turning, for having no longer any propriety they retain nothing for themselves, and return directly to God all the glory of what He does in them and by them as a perfume of an excellent odor. Now he whom God *chooses* to help others, in receiving from Him the odor of His *perfume,* is truly *holy,* since possessing nothing in himself, he must necessarily be filled with God, and consequently be holy.

These words, *Oh sons of Levi!* Uttered by inspiration, denoted the grief that Moses had for these souls more than all the others, for being more advanced their fault is the less pardonable. It is as if he said to them, Oh! Ye who were destined to perform what I do, ye who were to have been soon introduced therein, ye who have been marked out for these divine employments, how have ye (done such a thing when ye ought to have recognized your dignity as much superior to that of the others! This manner of speaking equally makes known Moses' gentleness and charity, and his discernment.

8. Moses said also to Korah, Hear me Sons of Levi.

9. Does it seem to you a small thing that the God of Israel has chosen you from all the   people, and has made you come near him to serve him in the ministry of the tabernacle, and has employed you in his sacrifices in presence of all the people?

He addresses himself principally to Korah as the author of this faction, and by him to all the others that might be in the same degree with him. Moses then is pained at their fault, because the state from which he saw them fallen was so elevated above that of the others, and he reproaches them so simply and justly, "But *did it seem* too *little* for you *that* the *God* of souls *had separated* you from everything common and earthly, that He had cut off from you all that could hinder His most intimate communications, *that he had* afterwards *made you come near him to serve him in the tabernacle,* that is to say, to sacrifice to Him in the center of yourselves, and also to serve Him in this state in the things of the interior only, *by* which He was disposing you for afterwards aiding souls? He did more, for you had already the power of helping them by your sacrifices and prayers, and you were as mediators between God and the people."

10. Has he made you come near him, you and your brethren the children of Levi, that you may aspire to the sovereign priesthood also?

Has the Lord bestowed upon you so many graces, *on you and on all the sons of Levi who* are in a like degree with you, that you may aspire to be *sovereign priest,* wishing to mix yourselves with the giving of the divine oracles, which is the final state of the shepherd and to which you have not yet been called, and daring to attribute to yourselves by a great crime what is only due to God, even to meddling in a thing for which He has not chosen you, for in order to be the oracle of God it is necessary to be annihilated so as to mix therein nothing of one's own, and to say only what God says.

> *31. Hardly had Moses ceased speaking when the earth opened under their feet.*

> *32. And the earth opened her mouth and swallowed them up with their tents and all that belonged to them.*

This is the punishment merited by those who of themselves put their hands to what God does not desire of them, and who desire to be conductors of others through presumption and self sufficiency, namely, *that the earth* which seemed to be *under their feet,* that is to say, all the earthly things which they seemed to have trodden under foot and to have been far above, and all sensualities, *re-open* and receive them into their womb. Then they are overwhelmed by the very things they had surmounted, and this earth and sensuality engulf them even to *their tents,* denoting the place of repose, showing that the center and the will are enveloped in this fall.

> *35. At the same time there came a fire from the Lord and consumed the two hundred and fifty men who offered incense.*

But *the fire* of love *which comes from God* and tries all things and all works, burning what is combustible, and sparing what is not, *consumed these men* who desired to do what God asked not of them, for all

122

their works merited fire, being only proprietary works, as says St. Paul, that "the fire will try each man's work." But the works of pure love, being exempt from all propriety, cannot be consumed, and their fire burns only for God, being consumed for His glory, whilst the others being proprietary are consumed by the fire of propriety and cupidity, which, robbing God of what is due to Him, attracts *the fire* of His wrath and not that of His love, for the fire of love remounts speedily to Him from whom it came, with the same purity with which it set out, but the fire of justice does not re-ascend until it has consumed the propriety opposed to it.

CHAPTER XVII.

8. Moses found that Aaron's rod; which was for the house of Levi, had budded, and that the buds were blown, the flowers sprung up, which, as the leaves spread, were changed into almonds.

God causes *Aaron's rod to flower,* to serve as a perpetual sign that it is necessary to be like it to become an apostle. *His rod had budded,* that is to say, out of its substance there had sprung a germ of life. This is what is done when, from the mystic ashes, as from a dead wood, there is reproduced a new life by the interior resurrection. But it is not enough for this rod to bud (denoting that it has resumed life again and is full of sap), it must, moreover, *flower* (which is a more advanced state after the resurrection), *and bear fruit,* and its leaves must spread out, meaning that the soul is placed a: large, so that its works are no longer restrained, and in fine its *fruits* must become ripe. All this admirably represents the interior seasons of a soul in as advanced a state as this. After winter, the time of the mystic death—just as this rod was dead—spring resuscitates and causes it to bud and blossom; summer forms the fruits and gives them increase; and autumn brings them to maturity. This is a very visible picture of the resurrection of the soul in God; its renewal in Him; its confirmation in this state; and its outward extension in perfect freedom, and with the fruits of the season serving as nourishment and sustenance for other souls.

> *9. Moses brought out all the rods from before the Lord, and showed them to the children of Israel, who recognized them; and each tribe took its own.*

> *10. And the Lord said unto Moses, bring back Aaron's rod into the tabernacle of the covenant, that it may serve as a sign to the rebellious children of Israel.*

The Lord desires this *rod to be kept* (representing the authority and power that these apostolic persons have over those submitted to them), as *a mark* of the state in which those ought to be who are called to the guidance of others. It is necessary, I say, that they have flowers and fruits in maturity, and their leaves all spread out, before attempting to lead.

CHAPTER XVIII.

20. The Lord said unto Aaron, Thou shalt possess nothing in their land, and thou shalt have no inheritance among them. I myself shall be thy portion and inheritance in the midst of the children of Israel.

O happy *portion* that of apostolic souls! Whatever *inheritance* of holiness the others may have, it is a holiness mingled with *earth* and propriety; but as for the heritage of the *house of* Levi, which is that of apostolic persons, there is no longer anything for them, neither in heaven nor in earth. God alone is *their inheritance;* God is their portion and their possession; and God is to them all things in such a manner that He alone moves them and acts in them. They claim nothing, and have no inclination for anything whatsoever, for they possess the same inheritance that is possessed in heaven, namely, God Himself; and most really, although yet under the vail of faith. Souls who do not permanently possess God are continually desiring, looking for, or sighing for something or other in the degree of their estrangement, but the former souls have no longer any tendency or inclination. They are in expectation of nothing, not even of eternity, for they possess, in an excellent manner, the God of eternity; and possessing the Sovereign Good, nothing is wanting to them, and it is on this account that they no longer desire anything.

But it will be said, should these persons not earnestly desire at least not to lose God by sin ? Ah! If they could still think of that, they would be occupied with their own interests, and with something less than God. Thus they would not be in the state whereof I speak, in which we repose in God through a perfect *abandon,* without care or uneasiness about what concerns us. It belongs to God to prevent them from offending Him, and they could not be occupied with anything out of Him, however holy it might be, without coming out of their state of loss in God. Whoever says loss means more than a thousand oblivions. It is possible sometimes to recollect something that has been forgotten, but what is wholly lost can never be refound. That which has only strayed can be found, but what has been lost in God cannot be found without coming out of God. Thus, if this soul could think or fear of losing what it possesses, or could look by itself on what it possesses, by this very thing it would issue from its state as long as these dispositions subsist. God alone and nothing else.

It will be said to me again, that if this soul has some care, it is for the glory of God. To this I reply, that it is incapable of thinking of the glory of God out of Him. God's glory is Himself; this is sufficient without its being able to think of it. The whole business of this soul is to no longer exist. God is its glory; it is His to provide for it. This is not the business of this creature, which has no more occupation, for it is not.

CHAPTER XX.

4. The people said to Moses and Aaron, Where-
fore have you brought all the multitude of the Lord
into this desert, that we and our cattle should die
there?

5. We can sow nothing; there are no figs, nor vines,
nor pomegranates, and what is worse, there is not
even water to drink.

This encampment of the people in the desert of
Zin signifies advancement in the desert of faith, which
appears so much the poorer as it is the more purified,
for the soul loses its supports the more, and everything that could give it some assurance out of God.
This soul bewails its poverty, beholding itself stripped
of the best things, even to no longer being able to make
use of the most excellent *fruits* of the church, namely,
the sacraments and holy practices. *There is,* it says, *no*
place where we can sow, since we can do no works by
ourselves. The church seems to have no more fruits
for us since we are deprived of all it has of the most
holy, the sacraments (from which God well knows how

to wean souls when He desires to carry their stripping further). For us there are *neither figs* (signifying the sweetness found in doing good works); *nor vines,* which would enable us to taste of the grapes of virtues; *nor pomegranates* (representing charity by their fruits). We appear deprived of all these great goods. Moreover, *there is no water,* the water of all sensible grace being dried up for us.

3. Would to God we had perished with our brethren before the Lord.

It is then that there are felt the pains of death. *Why did we not die,* say they, in our abundance? This is what is said every time they enter a new desert and a more denuded state: for *it* must be observed that each state has its degrees, and each degree a beginning, progress, and end. Thus the country of faith is long, and one passes there from desert to desert, from nakedness to nakedness, and the last desert is always the more terrible, so that one comes Out of one stripping to enter into another, the latter appears always new, and the preceding one seemed even to have great blessings compared with the poverty of that which follows. And what is strange, those who have attained to this point, although they have received so many graces, and have seen so many miracles performed on their behalf, can never be persuaded that they will arrive at the end. And as, when they are in the repose of the union of the faculties—although this is but the beginning of faith—they fancy themselves at the end, and think not that there is anything else to possess; so when they are in naked faith, and in this stripping, they do not believe

132

they will come out of it, and think not of going on to the end. It is the quality of the little courageous to be cast down by the slightest obstacles, and to despair of the enterprise where they think they cannot succeed.

7. The Lord said unto Moses,

8. Take thy rod and gather together the people, thou and Aaron thy brother, and before them speak to the rock, and it will give forth water.

9. Moses took the rod which was before the Lord, as he had commanded him.

God seeing that this people have not strength enough to pass so bare a state, commands Moses to *speak to the rock,* for it was time for this people that the rock should *give forth water,* since all must drink of the living water of this rock before entering into other states, as has been said before (Gen. xxix. 3). This living *water* drawn *from the rock* is the grace merited by Jesus Christ, who forms the refreshment of those who are in this desert, through the conformity they have with his states, not by thoughts, sight, or light of them, but by a real resemblance, although imperceptible, God hiding it from the soul in order to make it walk with more faith, and consequently with more purity. Now here it is no longer necessary to use the *rod* in order to strike, for *speech* is sufficient to cause this water to come, which is Jesus Christ; since being the speech of the Father, this same speech only was necessary to communicate it to these souls.

It is for this reason that apostolic persons produce it in souls by speech, and not by the rod of direction; for it is no longer their authority that acts here, but the divine infusion shed abroad by them by means of speech. This is why Jesus Christ has not desired to reproduce Himself in His Sacrament by other means than that of speech, for speech alone can produce the Word, who is the speech of the Father, and whom the Father produces in speaking.

It is then in faith that the soul enters into conformity with Jesus Christ, without thinking of Him as distinct from it, nor looking upon this relation. In the passivity of light there are given many knowledge's of Jesus Christ, which nourish and recreate the soul; but here it has no light of Jesus Christ, and although it never was more like Him, yet it never perceived Him less. It continues to enter into His states by a true conformity, without thinking of it however, bearing them all entire until by Jesus Christ Himself it arrives in God alone, where it will be hid with Him, until it has the power of reproducing Him, and, as it were, incarnating Him anew in souls by its word. For the soul having become God in some manner by participation, has the power of the speech of God, which is entrusted to it to cause the Word to be born in others. Speech essential produces the Word-God in Himself, and speech substantial, received into the soul, produces the Word in others. I will explain myself. God, from all eternity, begets His Word by His speech, and in time, His same speech in Jesus Christ produced the same Jesus Christ in the holy sacrament. Thus this divine speech, out of the mouth of an annihilated soul (although then it is only mediate and not substantial), who performs the office of priest for interior communications, produces the Word in the souls to whom it speaks; and this is why so many conversions are made by the simple speech of these persons. This is clear in St. Paul, who says, "my little children whom I bring forth again with pain until Jesus Christ be formed in you." It is by speech, without doubt, that he brings them forth to the Savior, as he clearly says in another place, "I have begotten you in Jesus Christ through the gospel;" and it is by this very speech that Jesus is formed in us, God rendering it powerful and efficacious to carry Him into hearts, and to make them conform to Himself.

> *10. Moses gathered together the multitude of the people before the rock, and said to them, Hear now ye rebels and unbelievers, believe ye that we can fetch water out of this rock?*
>
> *11. And raising his hand he struck the rock with his rod, and the water came out abundantly, so that all the people and cattle drank of it.*

This is a fault usually committed by those who conduct, namely, not to be content with the simple word of God, which is given them according to the want of souls at the moment they consult them. They always wish to use, as formerly, old methods and general maxims of direction, and the more they have seen them succeed well, the more they cling to them. But this is a thing extremely displeasing to God, as much because He desires to be the absolute director of the directors themselves, as because He alone knows the wants of souls according to the designs He has over them. Therefore the apostolic conductor must, in all things, give himself up to the movement of the Spirit of God.

This shortcoming is here visible in *Moses,* and however perfect he was, God permitted him to fall into this infidelity for the instruction of other directors. As he had been accustomed to perform great wonders by striking *with his rod,* and that had never failed him, he wished to do the same here in order to draw water from the rock. But God not having commanded it, although He had ordered him to take the rod in his hand as a sign of his authority of direction, he added of himself *the striking of the rock,* of which God had not spoken. He even doubted that it was not sufficient to speak to the rock if he did not strike it also, to perform this great miracle; and thinking he did well, he mixed together the work of God and his own operation.

Moses' fault was this, that having been told by God to take his rod, but to *speak* to the rock, in place of speaking he struck it, and thus did not glorify God, which he would have done had he used speech alone. The reason why it displeased God was, that he desired to show before the eyes of the whole people that what was of the old must pass away, and thus to take away from them all support in this miraculous rod. In fact, from this time Moses' rod did no more miracles. The second reason was, that God wished to make known that Jesus Christ was to perform all His miracles by speech, He who was the Father's word, and that there was to issue from Him, as from a living rock, torrents of grace which He was to shed abroad upon the people. Miracles belong more to the old law than to the new. Thus Jesus Christ seeing that the people being accustomed to miracles were influenced in their faith almost entirely by them, came to teach us the secret of faith, which must rely purely and simply upon His speech.

> *12. And the Lord said unto Moses and Aaron, Because ye believed me not, to glorify me before the children of Israel, ye shall not bring this people into the land that I will give them.*

It is strange that a little fault, or a leaning on anything whatsoever in souls so advanced, should be punished so rigorously; and that God should show Himself so angry at it! He does not, however, take away their grace, nor cause them to come out of their state. He does not say to them, ye shall not enter into the promised land, since Moses having had the essential communication, and having seen God face to face, had nothing more to possess for himself; and being in God in so eminent a manner, he could not enter into an inferior state: but God says to him, *ye shall not bring this people into the land which I will give them,* thus showing that He took away from him from that time the supreme grace and perfect success of direction; and that although he had himself passed into the states leading to the most consummate perfection that can be attained in this life, he would not however have the advantage of conducting his flock to the perfection of its origin.

It is thus that God punishes the directors who desire to mingle their own industry with His word, for this industry can indeed cause the water of grace to flow, but cannot give the living water of Jesus Christ, and produce it in souls—this industry hindering this divine production, which the Word of God alone can produce, and that all alone. God also complains here that this infidelity has prevented Him from being *glorified before the people,* as he would have been, if without striking the rock His word alone had been trusted.

> *25. The Lord said unto Moses, Take Aaron, and his son with him, and bring them to Mount Hor.*

> *26. And strip Aaron of his garments, and put them upon Eleazar, his son.*

God *takes from Aaron his priestly decorations,* in order to divest him of the character of his priesthood, and to degrade him. But this is the figure of the stripping of the spirit of direction. This is a common punishment for those who conduct others and commit like faults. God afterwards gives this spirit of direction to others, for it is never lost. He no sooner takes it *away* from him who loses it through his infidelity, than he *puts it upon* another, and often *one of his spiritual children.*

14. At that time Moses sent messengers to the king of Edom, saying,

17. Let us pass, I pray thee, through thy country.

18. The king replied, I will not let thee pass by my country. If thou comest there. I will go out with my army against thee.

21. Therefore Israel withdrew from him,

Often interior souls would do good in some *countries*, and dwell or pass there for that purpose; but the demon, seeing the great fruit that these souls produce in those they converse with, *opposes* with all his might this passage. He *arms* everything to hinder it, and blinding people, he leads them to *refuse* themselves their own good fortune. It is surprising how much is done to hinder these souls from having any communication in the monasteries. The princes of the church arm themselves against them without knowing them. Slander deploys all her arrows, and the world comes with armed hand against these persons, who think not of defending themselves, desiring only to do good. Therefore God often makes His people take another road, or sometimes He arms Himself, and combats so as to make a passage for them; or He even casts the former out from their pulpits and thrones to establish His servants in their place.

Chapter XXI.

1. And when king Arad the Canaanite heard that the people of Israel were come by the way of the spies, he gave battle against them, and having gained the victory, he carried off a great booty.

It happens often and almost always that God, by a stroke of His providence, makes use of the creatures to strip these souls of their *booty*. This booty is the honor and self-esteem that they have of themselves, and also what others have of them. They lose then all the esteem of the creatures, that being a good that must be destroyed. For it is not enough to be guilty of a thousand weaknesses towards God, which render us criminal both in His eyes and our own, as happened so many times to this people; but they must also appear the same in the eyes of men, and our infamy must be known to all. This is what happens when the creatures carry off our spoils, triumphing over our loss. It is then that people say, behold this abandoned people whom God sustained! He has made them fall into the hands of their enemies. Thus the creatures who overwhelm this interior people by slander, enrich themselves with their *booty*, taking occasion to boast that their way is much superior, and that it is far better to act as they have done, with energy and prudence, than to proceed by this *abandon.*

> *2. But Israel vowed a vow unto God, and said to him, If thou wilt deliver this people into our hands we will destroy their cities.*

> *3. And the Lord heard the prayer of Israel, and delivered up the Canaanites to them; and they utterly destroyed them, and razed their cities to the ground.*

But *Israel,* or the abandoned souls, have no sooner shown God by a new *abandon* that if they ever again return to their first reputation, they will retain nothing for themselves, and that they will take good care to appropriate nothing; on the contrary, that they *will destroy the cities* in which self-love is fortified. They have no sooner, I say, witnessed their readiness to do this, than God gives them the advantage over their enemies. The Lord destroys them by a blow of His hand, and at the same time brings to view the malignity of slander, and the innocence of His people.

> *4. The people were wearied by reason of the length of the way, and felt faint because of the labor.*

> *5. And they murmured against God and Moses, saying, Wherefore have ye brought us out of Egypt to die in this wilderness? We have here neither bread nor water, and this light nourishment is loathsome to us.*

There happen similar weaknesses almost the whole length of the desert of faith, because of its obscurity. Feeble souls *weary are disgusted*, and afflicted; they say continually that *so light a bread tires them*, that is to say, so spiritual a food. But God, wishing to save this people and not to destroy them, punishes them immediately for their weaknesses.

> *6. Therefore God sent fiery serpents among the people, and they bit the people and made many of them die.*

He *sends serpents* whose envenomed tongues sting them, and give them *mortal wounds*. These thrusts of poisoned tongues are a thing hard to bear, and so much the more severe as those who suffer them, feeling themselves guilty of many things, bear all the confusion of them both outwardly and inwardly, both before God and men.

> *7. And they came to Moses and said to him, we have sinned in murmuring against you and against the Lord, pray unto him that he take away these serpents from us. And Moses prayed for the people.*

Then these poor souls, all in confusion, frankly confess *that they have sinned*, and that it is by their own fault that they have drawn down upon themselves this just punishment. That if they are not guilty of what is insinuated against them they are so of many other things. They go then to their director and tell him that they know their own wretchedness, all that has happened to them and what they deserve, but that they cannot do anything either in withdrawing themselves from their weaknesses, or in delivering themselves from these wounds, but that he can accomplish with God what he wills. Then *he prays* for these afflicted souls, and God instructs him as to the means to employ to cure their wounds.

> *8. The Lord said to him, Make thee a serpent of brass, and set it up on a high place and every one that is hurt that looketh upon it shall not die.*

God commands a *serpent of brass to be made,* for the remedy of this evil must be found in the evil itself. This serpent was *of brass,* brilliant as fire and thus resembling those who gave the children of Israel these *burning* wounds. Nothing so much causes the soul to die to itself, and draws it so greatly from the chagrin and ennui of the road as the sight of its feeblenesses and the remembrance of what is said of it. This much advances its death. For when weaknesses are not followed by slander it passes more lightly, but when slander awakens the remembrance of the terrible state we bear, it renews the pain and renders the thing unbearable.

The *sight of the serpent* raised by the command of God, which is the mark of His will, calms and *cures,* as also does the union with what Jesus has suffered, when the soul can look upon it, which God sometimes causes to happen, giving it suddenly, and in the light of faith which passes as a spark, a simple view of His crucified and outraged Son. At other times He awakens in the center of the soul the love of the cross, and this restores life to it. Whoever has the experience of this will confess that it is as true as it is beautiful, and that it is really experienced in souls as it is depicted under the veil of these figures, although apparently they may seem to be far removed from it.

> *33. Og, king of Bashan came with all his people before the Israelites to fight against them.*

> *34. And the Lord said unto Moses, Fear him not, for I have delivered him into thy hand.*

> *35. And he was defeated with all his sons, and all his army passed under the edge of the sword until all were slain.*

God delivers up to these souls Og, who is the demon, *with all his people*, for far from being subjected to him they rule over him, and they would not even fear though all hell should be armed against them, not that they believe they have the power of conquering him, of this they do not think, but it is Our Lord who has vanquished him for them, and they have conquered in Him, so that now, without any labor on their part, they find themselves freed from these enemies who even fly before them. These souls with one word, and by their approach alone, cast down the demons, for the Lord *has delivered them into their hands*.

CHAPTER XXII.

5. Balak, King of Moab, said to Balaam,

6. Come and curse me this people for they are mightier than I.

12. God said to Balaam, Go not with them, and curse not this people for I have blessed them.

Is it not today that people desire to make the prophets, that is to say those who fill the place of God, speak against His interior people, and too often there are found some of these persons feeble enough to *allow* themselves to be won over. But God, who is master of all, knows well how to prevent it. *This* interior *people* is *stronger* than all the others, for their strength lies not in their arms nor in their own defense but in God.

28. The Lord opened the mouth of the ass, *and it spoke.*

Often although the will of man be determined upon a cowardly action against the interior people, when it is on the point of being executed God causes quite the opposite to be *done* and *said.*

> *31. God also opened Balaam's eyes and he saw an angel standing in the way and holding a naked sword i his hand, and falling on his face he worshipped.*

Then the animal and exterior part finding itself powerless to execute what is desired of it, is the cause of the soul *opening its eyes* to see the danger to which it was exposed, which obliges it at the same time to do quite contrary from what it had resolved.

CHAPTER XXIII.

7. Balaam said,

*8. How shall I curse whom God hath not cursed?
How shall I defy whom the Lord hath not defied?*

This is the manner of speaking of those persons who are enlightened by their faults, as Balaam himself afterwards confessed that it was by his fall that his eyes were opened. They remain after that intrepid, changing nothing of what is God's order, blessing what they are desired to *curse,* and exposing their life for the defense of the truth.

9. This people shall dwell alone, and thy shall not be mingled amongst the nations.

They *shall* always *dwell alone,* although in the midst of all the world, for their heart being separated from it they are always alone with God. Therefore they are not reckoned amongst the nations, not being a people of the earth but the chosen people of God, and reserved only for Him.

10. Who can count the dust of Jacob, and know the number of the generation of Israel? Let me die the death of the just, and let my last end be like theirs.

This man, established in the truth through his fault, knows well the advantages of the interior persons. His manner of speaking so well expresses that of a soul returned from its wandering, and which has a sincere regard for those it wished to afflict. *Who can count,* says he, *the dust* of this people? He compares it to dust on account of the innumerable multitude promised to Jacob under the same simile.

But this also means the humiliations that this people must bear, which will be but *dust* in appearance, but which will be an innumerable dust and will compose the people of God. *Who can know the number* of their virtues and all the graces which God bestows upon them?

Oh how happy they will be *at death!* Since they will be then so much the more elevated in glory as they are now abased. Oh that I may *die the death of the just!* It is this death which fears nothing, for they are just from the justice of God, not being able to attribute to themselves anything of all God has placed in them, but abandoning all, and regarding it in Him alone. All the justice of man is but filthiness before Him; as Isaiah has clearly expressed it, "All the works of our justice are but as filthy rags." *Oh that my end might be like to theirs!* Oh that like them I may be stripped of all self-righteousness, to have only the righteousness of God! Then would my death be like unto theirs, seeing that by this stripping of all righteousness man is placed in his end.

> *19. God is not as a man that lie should he, nor as the son of man that he can repent. Will he not do then what he has spoken? And will he not fulfill what he has resolved upon?*

> *20. I have been brought to bless, and I cannot turn away this blessing.*

This addition to what has been already said shows how the justice of man is varying and *changeable,* but that which comes from God is not, and *can never lie;* therefore those whom God has clad with His justice can never incur His curse, for then He would curse what is His own. To be cursed of God they would require to lose first His justice, rebecoming proprietary without which they remain immovable in their blessing.

> *21. There is no idol in Jacob, nor statue in Israel. The Lord his God is with him, and the cry of the king's victory resoundeth in him.*

By *idols* is understood propriety, which is banished from the interior people; and by *statues* is denoted lying, which covers itself with the mantle of truth. This interior people then is as much removed from disguise and duplicity as it is removed from propriety. The love of ourselves gives birth to lying, and pure charity is the mother of truth. *In this* innocent *people,* then, *there is found neither* propriety nor lying. Therefore *the Lord* their God *is with them,* not being able to be separated from a soul no longer proprietary. For He Himself fills up the void caused by it's renouncing its propriety.

It is on this account that a *cry of victory re-sounds in them,* because existing of themselves no longer, and God alone being in them as Sovereign King whom nothing resists, this cry of the *King's victory,* causes itself to be heard *in them.* Observe it is the King's victory and not the victory of the people, and that this king is not out of this people, but in the midst of them. Oh beautiful difference! So long as man can work by his own efforts, and fight with his own arms, the victory is attributed to him. When God walked be-fore him it was said that the Lord fights for him, and walks at his head. At that time the union is yet only in the faculties. There still remain some enemies whom God Himself destroys, the soul being passive to His operation. But here the cry of the King's victory is continual in this soul; God having taken possession of its center, He is victorious king, and this center chants unceasingly the *victory of its king.* It even makes it *resound* by great *cries,* for there are no more combats to sustain. When the union is yet only in the faculties, although God is victorious, walking at the head of the army, it always costs something, and the victory is of-ten gained only after some wounds. But here it is not the same; the victory is without combat, and it is per-manent and durable, as the Sovereignty of God in this soul is immoveable.

*23. Surely there are no augurs in Jacob, nor sooth
sayers in Israel. It will be told in their time to Jacob
and Israel what God hath wrought.*

The augurs and soothsayers denote those who
are in the state of light, infinitely inferior to this state,
since then the soul yet possesses itself. Oh how far
removed that is from the state of faith and perfect
abandon! When it will be recognized, either during
the day of the same faith or in eternity. *This people*
(who have been conducted by the way of faith and abandon), *will be told* with admiration of the marvels *God
has wrought* in them. This expression points to a great
astonishment, as it is said in the book of Wisdom, that
the wicked, beholding the just saved with so much glory,
will be seized with amazement, and troubled with a great
fear, saying to themselves, madmen that we were! Their
life appeared to us folly, and their death shameful, yet
behold them raised to the rank of children of God, having their lot with the saints.

*24. Here is a people that will rise up like a lioness,
and lift themselves up like a lion.*

This disappropriated *people rise* with boldness
like the lion and *lioness.* They elevate themselves by
the movement of their faith and interior state, for it is
founded on God, who is the highest elevation they can
attain to. They are so assured of their victory that they
can fear nothing, for all their strength is in the lion,
even of the tribe of Judah; and having become one with
Him, *they rise* up *like* Him, invested, as He is, with the
strength of God.

153

*25. He shall not lie down until he eat of the prey,
and drink the blood of the slain.*

He shall not lie down in death, nor by any
feebleness, *until he has eaten his prey,* that is to say,
until he has devoured all the bitternesses and obstacles
he may encounter. Although the soul be advanced in
the mystic life, and may have been stripped of many
things, and of the property of its own strength, there
yet remains to it another propriety; it is, that it appro-
priates to itself God's strength, and this usually happens. We know that we are stripped of our proper
strength, but we find ourselves yet strong in God; but
expecting nothing of ourselves, through the convic-
tion we have of our nothingness, we look for much
from God, by a subtle desire that this void should be
filled by Him. But the true annihilated one existing no
longer, has neither strength in himself; nor in God; but
God alone is strong, God alone is mighty, God is everything. This is a degree much further advanced.

Now this soul being thus raised again by the
resurrection, and reclad with the strength of God, *will
lie down no more* through sin, and even it shall not die
until it has *devoured its prey,* namely, what remains to
suffer in the states through which it must yet pass, in
order, from strength in God, to arrive at the strength
of God. There are no more victories to gain, but there
are things to be eaten and *devoured.* It is no longer a
thing that is to be destroyed. No, it is something that
must pass into us, and must necessarily be swallowed.
We must *drink of the blood,* even to the last drop,

without allowing anything to escape. Ah! If one could express what that means, but it could not be comprehended. I pray the souls that are at this stage not to spare themselves, and not to fall away or resume themselves in anything. For they must consummate all God's will, however horrible it may appear, as one is horrified at drinking blood; so that it may be said, imitating Jesus Christ, "Holy Father, I have finished the work that Thou hast given me to do;" and the more that these persons will devour and consume these things, the more God will swallow up and consume them in Himself.

It is necessary to eat and devour the whole will of God, and suffer ourselves to be watered by all bitternesses, before being devoured by God, and passing into Him by a state of transformation. It is necessary that the will of God should be passed entirely into ourselves, and become, as it *were,* natural to us (as what one eats and drinks is changed into our substance), before God eats us. God's eating is the reception of the soul into him—the finishing of its annihilation by its consummation into Himself, which is as the digestion of things eaten. Then this devoured and digested soul, radically annihilated, passes in its substance by transformation into God alone, where it dwells in Him, lost for ever. Then there remains only God alone, in perfect essential Unity, and the personal Trinity in its operations, as much outwardly as inwardly, as was said before (chap xvi. 3).

CHAPTER XXIV.

1. Balaam, seeing that it was God's will that he should bless Israel, went no more as formerly to seek auguries, but turned his face towards the desert.

2. And lifting up his eyes he saw Israel reposing in their tents, according to their tribes, and the spirit of God came vehemently upon him.

Persons who have recognized the goodness of the passive way, and have already entered therein, are yet some time in seeking lights represented by *things divined,* that is to say, perceptible, as if they desired some knowledge of the future; but whenever they comprehend that the most ample blessings of God are for the people who walk in faith, then without going any more to seek for these lights, they *turn themselves* to *the side of the desert* of faith. One can indeed turn towards this desert of one's-self, aided by grace; but we cannot enter therein except God introduce us. To turn one's-self towards the desert is nothing but to abandon one's-self to God, so that He may make us enter therein if it be His will, and to quit all our lights

157

procured and sought after, in order to remain in this stripping and *abandon,* waiting for God to do what it pleaseth Him.

It is then that this soul has *its eyes* opened to *see this people of* faith in the stripping and desert of naked faith, *reposing in their tents,* that is to say, in this same nakedness of faith; for there is a great difference between being in tents and reposing in them. We are in the tent when we are introduced into the desert of faith; but we only repose there when we are far advanced in this same faith, so that we *dwell* there without difficulty and are content.

This people then rested in their tents *according to their tribes,* that is, each according to his degree; seeing that there is no state that does not contain several degrees, some being more advanced, and others less so, according to God's design and their faithfulness: for it is certain that of many souls who walk in the same ways, some are much more advanced than others.

Now, when this interior man, depicted here under the figure of *Balaam,* had abandoned himself to enter into the way of faith, quitting all his distinct and perceptible lights, immediately *the spirit of God came upon him with vehemence,* that is to say, It came with impetuosity to conduct the soul, which being willing to allow itself to be stripped of all natural and acquired light, of all seeking after supernatural knowledges, abandons itself to It without reserve; from that moment It seizes upon it, and becomes its only mover.

> *4. Thus saith he who has heard the words of God, and who has seen the vision of the Almighty, he who falleth and his eyes are opened.*

Man is no sooner stripped of his own lights, and reclothed with the Spirit of God, than he is placed in truth; and it is then he is in a fit state *to hear the words of God,* which are words of truth taking away everything from the creature and attributing all to God. Then also he sees *the vision of the Almighty.* He does not say that he saw in vision the Almighty, but that he saw the vision of the Almighty, this state here being above visions, and even above the sight of the power of God out of God; but he saw *the vision of the Almighty,* which means that he saw things as God sees them, and in the truth of God Himself, who knows His sovereign power and the infinite feebleness of the creature; in fine, he recognizes in an indistinct manner the all of God and the nothingness of the creature.

Scripture also observes that it was *by the fall that his eyes were opened.* Oh happy fall, producing so many goods, and which, drawing souls out of their pride, opens their eyes to see their own feebleness and the strength of God!

> *5. How beautiful are thy pavilions, Oh Jacob, and thy tents, Oh Israel !*

He continues to show how his eyes have been opened to the truth. *How beautiful are thy pavilions,*

Oh Jacob; as if he said, oh perfect *abandon* (represented by Jacob), how lovely are thy pavilions! For these pavilions are no other than the repose in *abandon*, which is entire destitution. Oh what a beautiful thing is this state of destitution to those that know it! Not to issue out of one's *abandon* in the extreme trials through which we must pass is something; but not to come out of the repose in this *abandon* when these same things take place is what enraptures God's heart. This belongs to His servants; for it is quite possible to remain in *abandon* without being in repose, being, on the contrary, agitated by doubts and troubles, and pierced with mortal griefs: but to remain as well *in the repose* of this *abandon*, as in *abandon* itself is a rare perfection.

But if these pavilions of Jacob are so beautiful, *the tents of Israel* are not less so. *Israel*, as has been said, is the strength of God. Oh beautiful thing, to have lost all proper strength by the very experience of our weakness, and to have entered thus into the strength of God! But it is a much more beautiful thing to dwell *in repose* in this strength in the midst of all our feeblenesses. The more the soul sees itself miserable, the more it knows that it is only its God who is strong: this is a beautiful thing: but to remain in repose stripped of all strength, and covered with all weaknesses, being content that God alone is strong, without coming out of this repose to regard one's weakness and to wish to remedy it, glorifying thus by one's infinite weakness the infinite strength of God, this is what cannot be too much admired.

*6. As valleys filled with forests; as gardens by the
river's-side are well watered, so are the tents which
the Lord has established, and as cedar trees planted
near the waters.*

He compares, moreover, these souls *to valleys*,
because of their annihilation, but which are *full of forests*, seeing that the more they are void of themselves,
the more God fills them with His sublime communications. They resemble *the garden* of the Spouse, being *watered by the waters* of His grace; they are near
the rivers, for they approach the source, which is God,
their only origin. They are *as tents,* on account of their
great repose; but they are tents *which the Lord has set
up,* for this is a repose which He Himself has made
and continues to make, which is taken but in Him alone,
above everything mediate; and this is what renders it
invariable, depending no longer on anything subject to
change, but strengthened upon the Divine immobility.
They are in fine like cedars on account of the uprightness of their heart which has only God for its object,
and of the odour of their simplicity. For the qualities
of the cedar are to be perfectly straight and of a pleasant smell; and they are *planted near the waters,* since
candour and simplicity have always a gentle, fresh, and
agreeable air.

*7. The water will flow from his bucket, and his
seed shall extend like many waters.*

Out of the *reservoir* of this soul, which will be
filled from the source, there *will flow* a superabun-
dance of grace upon the others, who being inferior to

161

it will be aided and as it were watered by it. And *its* seed, the children of grace that God will give it, *shall spread as abundant waters,* which, dividing into a thousand branches, accomplish a thousand goods upon the earth.

> *8. God has brought him out of Egypt; his strength is like to that of the unicorn. This people shall eat up their enemies, they shall break their bones and pierce them with arrows.*

The *bringing out of Egypt* is the enfranchisement from propriety which reigns so powerfully in a carnal country. The *unicorn* is also a figure of the strength of God, as it is said in a psalm "With thy help shall we overturn our enemies, and by the power of thy name shall we tread on those that rise against us."

God having then taken away from this soul all propriety, and being Himself in it, consumes by His Divine power all that could harm it or prevent it from attaining its latter end. *To break their bones,* is to destroy self-love (its most dangerous *enemy)* even in substance; and to *pierce* its adversaries *with arrows,* is to exercise towards them an all-generous charity when even it is most ill-treated, confounding them so much the more as it renders them more good for the evil it receives; which is innocently to pierce them by the splendor of its virtues, as it is written, "The arrows of the little children have become their hurt, and the malice of their tongue has been turned against them."

*9. He couched, he slept like a lion, and like a lion-
ess that none dare awaken.*

It is then that it reposes and *sleeps like the lion
and the lioness,* being established in the repose of the
strength of God; and being permanently there, it comes
out no more, for neither demons, nor men, nor sin,
nor any creature *dare arouse it* from its repose in God
alone when thoroughly established therein.

*16.Thus hath he said, who falling has his eyes
opened.*

*17. I shall see him, but not now; I shall look upon
him, but not nigh. There shall be born a star from
Jacob, and there shall arise a sceptre out of Israel
which shall smile the princes of Moab, and destroy all the children of Seth.*

This person who *by falling has had his eyes
opened,* confesses that he *shall see* only *from afar*
what is to happen to these interior souls, as much because that can only be known in God, above everything
mediate, as because their consummation will be accomplished only by passing through impenetrable
states; and in fine it is not now the time for him to
know it. There will arrive a time when being dead to
himself, he shall behold it.

From this abandon carried to the point that
God desires, there *will spring the star of Jacob,* which
is the speech of God, producing the word when the
soul is transformed in God, as has been said. *And the*

sceptre shall arise out of Israel. This is the absolute power of the strength of God, and which will destroy everything that could hinder the production of Jesus Christ in souls, and this will be done by the same Jesus Christ, who is sceptre, star, speech, word, repairer, and destroyer of all opposing strength, who overturns and destroys all that leans upon the power of the creature, so that it will only be God's strength that is valiantly maintained, and it' will be maintained in souls through the same word by whom all things have been made.

23. Alas! Who shall live when God doeth these things?

24. The Hebrews even shall be destroyed at the end.

This man sighs grievously, recognizing these interior marvels yet distant from him, and knowing already that in order to see them wrought in himself by the power of God, it must cost him his life. Oh, he says, *who* can view God's operations, producing His word by the expression of His speech in souls, while there yet remains a breath of the self *life?* This is wholly impossible, since it is even necessary that the *Hebrews* of the Lord, and the holiest souls, *should perish at the end;* so that there may be but the reign of God alone.

Chapter XXV.

1. Israel dwelt then in Shittim, and the people began to commit whoredom with the daughters of Moab,

2. Who enticed them to their sacrifices, and they did eat of them, and worshipped their gods.

It is a strange thing that the most advanced souls, until they are permanently in God, can always sin. Amongst such holy souls there are yet found some cowardly enough to return to *idolatry,* which is, as I have said, the only sin (with that of lying) that they commit. But it is to be remarked that this happens to them only on account of conversing with strangers, attaching themselves willingly to multiplied persons, and even with the wicked, by natural friendships and by amusements, which bring them into the same way.

4. The Lord said unto Moses, Take of all the chiefs of the people, and hang them up against the sun, so that my fury may be turned away from Israel.

The fault being here voluntary, God causes *all the chiefs* to be punished for it, for it is the superior part that must bear the penalty. It is necessary that it should *be hanged upon a gibbet,* for God not willing to receive it, although already come out of its own land, it remains, after having resumed itself through its infidelity, *suspended* between heaven and earth; finding nothing upon earth to support it, for God does not permit it to rest there; and moreover, finding no access to heaven, which was the place of its repose and peace. By this suspension between heaven and earth, it suffers very great pain—the pain of purgatory, by which the soul, being out of itself; and not finding God to be received into Him, suffers a torment like to being hanged upon a gibbet, which cruelly afflicts it and suffocates it.

These chiefs of the people are hanged *against the sun;* because it is to be no longer propitious for them, and because they will find that its light striking them sharply on the eyes, will only serve to augment their pain. This is what happens to these fallen persons, who are still more afflicted by the remembrance of the favours they have received of God, and by the impression of His truth that remains to them.

Behold the punishment of souls who resume themselves and return to propriety in this degree— very different from the first penalty for idolatry, of which we have treated before (Exod.xxxii. 3). This punishment alone can *appease God,* and even cause the soul to re-enter a higher degree.

6. One of the children of Israel joined himself pub-
licly to a Midianitish prostitute.

7. And when Phinehas saw it, he rose up from
among the people and took a sword,

8. And pierced them both together; and the plague
with which the children of Israel were smitten, was
stayed immediately.

The cause of this kind of falls is voluntary reflection, and the desire of withdrawing from God to
return to one's self. Scripture calls this *fornication,*
for it is to take away one's self from God to give one's
self again to one's self, and this proprietary ME is no
other than an infamous carrion and villainous *prosti-*
tute, a rebel against God. But the generous director
comes to *slay* this sin *with his sword,* drawing the soul
out of its propriety; and this being done everything
ceases, since the propriety being destroyed, these persons can no longer suffer like pains, which they suffer
only from propriety, more or less, according as it is
more or less strong.

10. The Lord said unto Moses,

11. Phinehas, son of Eleazar, has turned away my
wrath from the children of Israel, in that he has
been zealous for my sake, so that I should not ex-
terminate the Israelites in my jealousy.

12. Say unto him, therefore, that I give unto him
the peace of my covenant.

13. And that the priesthood will be for him, and his seed of a surety for ever, for he hath been zealous for his God, and hath expiated the sin of the children of Israel.

It happens often providentially that some amongst the people, who were only to them as brothers, perform with regard to others the office of director, making known to them the cause of their misfortune, and tearing from them their propriety. Now as this is not done through a false zeal, nor to aspire to the direction, but only for God's glory, as Scripture declares and distinguishes it in a marked manner on behalf of Phinehas, there is merited by this the grace of general and ordinary direction. *I give him the priesthood,* saith the Lord; that is to say, I choose him director and apostle, *for he has been moved with my zeal;* and not his own. This has prevented Me from *consuming the children of Israel through my jealousy,* and for My own glory, seeing that Phinehas has himself espoused My interests, and has slain propriety.

God punished Korah and his adherents because they wished to meddle with the direction, seeking therein only their own glory, for the maintenance of which they desired to establish and preserve their self-love. But Phinehas is rewarded, because he puts his hand to correcting only through the movement of the spirit of God, and for His interests alone, and in consideration of his having slain self-love.

CHAPTER XXVII.

12. The Lord said also to Moses, Get thee up into this mountain Abarim, and there look upon the land which I will give to the children of Israel.

13. And when thou hast seen it, thou also shall go unto thy people, as Aaron thy brother has gone.

God still left Moses for sometime in this world to conduct His people in the desert; but on account of his infidelity God only lets him *see from afar off the promised land,* without his having the consolation of seeing his people established there in perfect security. He must *die, as well as Aaron,* the spirit of direction having been taken away from them on account of their infidelity, to be given to others

15. Moses answered God, saying,

16. Let the Lord, the God of the spirits of all men, set a man as chief over this multitude:

17. Lest the people of the Lord be as sheep without a shepherd.

He prays God without thinking of his own interests, being indifferent to everything, and perfectly content to die without introducing the people into the promised land. Such a soul can see nothing out of the will of God; and being stripped of all self-interest, it thinks only of the glory of the Lord and the interests of His children. Therefore he *prays* Him to appoint a person having His Spirit *to conduct this people* in what remains of the road until they have arrived in Him; otherwise, says he, these souls will wander like sheep without a shepherd.

> *28. The Lord said unto him, Cause Joshua the son of Nun a man in whom the spirit rests to come unto thee, and lay thy hands upon him.*

God told Moses to take him, into whom He had made *the spirit* of direction pass, and that he would conduct the people; but also *to lay his hands upon him* by a kind of consecration, in order to transmit to him what God wished to communicate of grace and discernment by his organism.

> *20. And thou shalt give him the necessary commands in presence of all, and a portion of thy glory, so that the whole multitude of the children of Israel may obey him.*

> *22. Moses did what the Lord had commanded him.*

Thou wilt finish explaining to him My will, and thou wilt leave him as an inheritance thy authority and *glory, so that he will be listened* to by all those whom he is to conduct.

Moses obeyed willingly, divesting himself not only of authority, but also *of the glory* he had acquired. Many souls, when far advanced, easily resign their authority to another; but there are not found so many willing to give up on behalf of others, the glory they have acquired in their government. If afterwards, those who conduct have great success, the former conductors attribute it to themselves, and desire it to be understood that it proceeds only from the things which were well commenced having been faithfully followed up; but if some misfortune should happen, that is thrown upon him who succeeds to the conduct, because, say they, he does not follow up well the footsteps of the former government. Oh how few there are who, stripping themselves of authority, equally strip themselves of the glory of it! It was in this that Moses was most faithful, and the example of all the faithful, for it is said, that *he did as the Lord had commanded him.*

Book III

DEUTERONOMY
WITH REFLECTIONS REGARDING
THE DEEPER CHRISTIAN LIFE.

Chapter I.

30. The Lord God, who is your guide, will himself fight for you, as he did in Egypt before your eyes.

31. In the desert ye have seen it yourselves, how the Lord your God has borne you in all the way that ye went, even as a man doth bear his young son, until ye came to this place.

God is the soul's guide so long as it is in the passive way, keeping Himself before it, and making it walk after Him. He *fights also for it* in this same state against all its enemies, to make a passage for it. But *in the desert* of faith have we not seen Him, all we who are there, or have passed it, Himself *carry* the soul *in His arms* (to make it redouble its speed) *as a father* (but a Father all full of tenderness and love) carries his little children? This expresses most perfectly the charity by which God carries souls (when they have abandoned themselves blindly into His hands) through all the so dark and painful ways through which it is necessary to pass to *arrive* at Himself, and be received in Him alone.

Again, this marks admirably how God's protection and assistance correspond to the various degrees of *abandon*. When the soul is only being born, God only begins to call it as from a distance, conducting under His orders this people by the medium of man and of direction, until it attains to the coming out of Egypt. When *abandon* is more advanced, God Himself comes to be its conductor; which appeared, when the people having entered into the desert, the Lord went before them in His cloud. But when *abandon* becomes most blind and most perfect, then God Himself takes this so dear a people *in His arms* and *carries them* with as much speed as safety into the true promised land, which is the transformation into Himself.

It must also be observed that, as it is natural where there is more assurance and signs, there is less faith and *abandon;* and that, on the contrary, where there is to be more faith and *abandon,* there must necessarily be less assurance and signs, so when *abandon* is yet feeble and imperfect, God does not do so much on behalf of souls, for they find plenty of supports out of Him. But in proportion as they blind themselves and detach themselves the more from everything to trust in Him alone, He makes them walk by more unknown ways, to exercise so much the more their faithfulness, and at the same time to take a more marvellous care over them, and in fine, when they seem to themselves to be quite lost, and being in a vast and frightful desert without any light of hope, one would say that everything failed them, and that so impenetrable paths can only end in their perdition, it is even then that God holds them in His arms and carries them with more speed and safety into Himself, enraptured that they hope in Him against all hope, and trust in Him without any appearance of success.

CHAPTER IV.

7. There is no other nation so great that it has gods so near to it as our God is nigh to us, and present to all our prayers.

It is certain that there is no other way in which the soul can have its *God so near it* as in this one, since He is more in it than itself, and it needs nothing else to make itself heard than to turn towards Him by a simple regard of amorous faith according to its degree.

12. Ye have indeed heard the voice of his speech, but ye have seen no figure.

We can indeed *hear* God's speech, which is His word, and even His *voice*, but we cannot *see* in Him any *figure* or image representing Him, for everything that presents a figure cannot be God. This is why there are so many mistakes in the way of lights and visions.

This also shows the necessity there exists for the stripping of all forms and images, whether sensible or intellectual, in order to arrive at pure contemplation and the intimate union, nothing sensible nor distinctly perceptible to the human spirit being sufficient to bring the soul into God, since He is infinitely above all that.

15. Ye saw no figure in the day that the Lord spoke to you in Horeb out of the midst of the fire.

16. Lest being seduced, ye make some idol to yourselves or some statue of man or woman.

For one true vision there arc a great number of false ones. The human mind pictures to itself many things, and the imagination forms images like to those that have been seen. Therefore in the way of faith these are no longer mentioned, because all the sensible is taken away from it to render it more pure, and because also these would amuse the soul and prevent it from advancing, keeping it always in itself in what is sensible and distinct, which is opposed to faith.

24. The Lord thy God is a consuming fire and a jealous God.

God is a consuming fire, leaving nothing proprietary in the creature without reducing it to ashes. When He comes into a heart He must destroy, consume, and annihilate everything else in it. *He is* also *a jealous God.* Oh if people knew what God's jealousy is, and how He desires no one with Him, however great and holy, it would terrify them! There is nothing that He does not set His hand to render Himself absolute master, and to destroy all the obstacles that prevent

180

Him from being so alone. He cannot agree with anything whatsoever, no virtue, no holiness can be found in company with Him. He is jealous; that is to say everything. And as He is the most worthy to be loved and faithful of all beloveds, He is also the most jealous and most ardent of all lovers. Therefore He calls Himself at the same time *a consuming fire,* so as to reduce to ashes all that is opposed to Him.

> *28. And there ye shall serve gods formed by men's hands.*

Moses announces to his people, that if they do not suffer themselves to be consumed by this fire, but desire to live on supports and figures, they *shall serve gods that are the works of men's hands,* that is, that they will be subjected to the labour of the active life to procure themselves good and holy things.

> *29. But if there ye shall seek the Lord your God, ye shall find him, if only ye seek him with all your heart and in all the affection of your soul.*

Nevertheless, he assures them, that in the midst of their activities they *shall find God,* provided, however, they *seek Him in their heart,* which is the place He desires to be found: but this will only be amongst all the crosses and afflictions that accompany this state; crosses, however, sweeter than all sweetnesses. It is in the heart that we must seek God with all our heart, and it is in thus seeking Him that we find the God of the heart.

32. Ask yourselves of the times that are past, which have been before you from the day the Lord created man upon the earth, and from one extremity of the heaven unto the other, if ever such a thing has been done or seen?

33. That a people should have heard the voice of God speaking to them out of the midst of the fire, as ye have seen and heard.

Scripture assures us that there is no other way than that of the interior, nor any other people than the abandoned people *who have* ever *heard the voice of God.* This voice is the Word; and it makes itself heard *out of the midst of fire,* for it issues out of the brazier of charity and pure love. The soul alone can hear this speech formed in the midst of this sacred fire, and which in burning the heart instructs it in the Divine verities.

35. So that ye might know that the Lord himself is God, and that there is none other than he.

Who are they that can hear Him and live? They are those who being mystically dead, are raised again to God, and made alive to die no more; for then they hear this word without dying; and this word which once caused them death, now procures them life. Now all these states take place, and are wrought so that the soul may know that it is *only God alone* that *is God,* and that there can be no true life out of Him.

CHAPTER V.

2. The Lord our God made a covenant with us at Horeb.

3. The Lord made not this covenant with our fathers, but with us, who are now alive.

This covenant which God had *made* with Moses and the people of Israel, and which *he did not make with their fathers,* shows the extent of the Divine power, and the magnificence of its bounty. For although He had raised Abraham, Isaac, and Jacob to His greatest favors and so high a perfection, and they had even given such authentic signs of their faith and love, yet they had not had so firm a covenant. This is the magnificence of my God, who could not elevate one creature so much, but He could yet discover Himself more to others. He measures not His so peculiar graces according to their merits, for who had been holier than these admirable patriarchs? Was not this people of Israel much inferior? Ah, it is to show His power so much the more that He takes pleasure in bestowing favors always greater and more reserved, often even much more to sinners than to great saints who have always lived in righteousness.

> *4. He has spoken with us face to face out of the middle of the flame, upon the mountain;*

> *5. And at that time I was the mediator and arbitrator between the Lord and you, to announce to you his word.*

As Moses was drawn from the peril of the waters, which was a kind of shipwreck, to be the conductor of so great a people, it happens likewise very often that God takes persons whom He has drawn out of the deeps of sin to make them signal conductors of souls. There is yet another reason for these so particular favors, and for this so close a covenant which God makes with Moses, and not with Jacob, Isaac, and Abraham: it is that these fathers and patriarchs were only called to the spiritual generation, and not to the office of shepherd; thus they had no need of so intimate an alliance, for it was not necessary for them to have so extended an experience of interior ways.

It must be observed that there are three kinds of souls—first, those to whom God gives a multitude of children, but far removed, and which are yet in the germ of their seed, as the Christians were contained in the blood of the martyrs: these are sanctified by God in Himself; as much as it is possible, having only designed them for this distant production; and He grants them out of His goodness a great number of children, of which they have but very little knowledge. There are others who do not bring forth in Jesus Christ, and yet continue to perform the office of preachers, and to aid souls already formed which God sends them, who gives them also the lights and knowledges necessary for this design, and instructs them in what to say. There are, lastly, others destined to beget souls, to bring them up, to conduct them in all the ways, and to bear them up to the most consummated state, God for this rendering them universal apostles, who bring forth, baptize, catechize, give milk and bread, and medicines according to need, and who, like Moses, conduct through the passage of the desert of faith, even to God.

It is to these great souls that God must give a double grace; and without regarding their demerits, He makes them enter into a real experience of everything, so that they may not only aid others by their lights, but even *bear them in their womb* by a veritable experience. To bear a soul in one's womb is to have experienced all that it suffers; therefore Moses said to the Lord (Num. xi. 12), "Have I brought forth all this great people whom I must bear in my womb?" God *makes,* then, with these persons the most particular and most intimate *covenant* that ever has been, for they are destined for generation and education, and bearing up to the consummation. Generation is accomplished by bringing souls out of Egypt, or multiplicity; education conducts them in the desert of faith; and consummation introduces them into the promised land, which is their end. It is, then, these souls that God unites to Himself in a closer manner than any other, showing Himself to them, face to face— that is to say, joining

Himself to them, face to face— that is to say, joining them to Himself; essence to essence, and at the same time placing them in the truth of that which He is, so that they may not be deceived in helping others.

But although God has made this essential union, He yet continues to make the father and shepherd walk by the way in which He conducts the others, sparing them in nothing, so that their experimental light may leave them neither doubt nor hesitation. For however enlightened a person may be, even in divine light, if he has not passed along all the way, he can never truly know what it is. The reason is, that one is apt to be deceived in the recital of things, and the tongue cannot sufficiently express what the soul experiences; more-over, the experience of others cannot make itself fully understood, nor place the soul that is conferred with, in the truth, because persons are different, and God never permits them to make known all that they are; so much the more as they do not well know themselves— above all, in the mystic states—in which their interior is much concealed and they can say less of it.

A person who has an evil similar to another's, will comprehend much better what it is, than he who, without having experienced it, only brings it to light, the light of experience being quite different from that of sight alone; as also those persons who have suf-fered the same evils, are more in a state to give the preservatives and remedies for them, and to know by what is told them of them, their beginning, their progress, and their end, and, in fine, the present state also serve as arbitrators and *mediators*—arbitrators, to decide clearly what is of the will of God; and mediators, to conduct souls to their last end.

> *24. The Lord our God has shown us his majesty and his glory. We have heard his voice out of the midst of the fire, and have seen today that, although God hath spoken to man, nevertheless man remaineth alive.*

God *shows His glory* to souls when they are in the passive way of light, He even *speaks* to them, *and they hear his voice out of the midst of the interior fire* which kindles them; but all this is wrought in leaving them their life. They have seen and heard all this, and yet *are still alive*, for these states here demand not the death of the soul, being graces proportioned to its capacity. They think, however, that being here they have passed through all the interior states; and, rejoicing in a living light, and in a great felicity, they persuade themselves that all the states of death of which they hear are either already passed for them, or are only chimeras; they are even offended, and make no difficulty in saying that they have arrived in God without having passed through the frightsome deserts and the most extreme trials of which they have been told something. Oh how greatly they deceive themselves, and how much difference there is between communications leaving life, and those that operate death.

The first *speech of God,* and the communications accompanying it, are graces acting in the faculties, which maintain the fire of love in the will, and ties, which maintain the fire of love in the will, and cause an increase of *life,* and not the death-blow; but the second word makes itself heard in the center, and it causes death; for it is this word that is *"the voice* of one crying in the wilderness: Prepare ye the way of the Lord, make his paths straight;" for it is God Himself who is to come, no longer by His gifts, but by Himself; and He must come not into the faculties, but into the center by the essential union. Now this word, which is to precede so great a state, must be a word of death, veritably causing the total death of the soul to itself, as it is necessary for the body to die in order for us to go to Heaven, and for it to rot and be raised again at the last day: for it is likewise necessary for the soul to die to everything in order to enter into Heaven, which is God Himself.

It is, then, in this light that the interior people said that the first word of God had not taken away their life, since they can hear it and also with it see *God's glory* and yet live.

> 25. *Why then shall we die, and will not this burning fire consume us? For if we hear once more the voice of the Lord our God, we shall die.*

Charity having reached a very eminent point, and its conflagration having become very great, it is necessary that this soul should die by the consummation of *this* very *fire,* which is no longer a moderate fire that can warm without reducing to ashes, as it did formerly, but which has increased so greatly that it must consume everything, and nothing escape it; there is no shelter from it, it is necessary to die; and if *God speaks* by this second word so burning, the soul must perish by its flame, which not only melts the soul (as the spouse once felt it), but makes it die and annihilates it. The figure of this is clearly enough expressed by St. Peter, who says, that "at the end of the world the elements shall melt with fervent heat, and the earth, and the works thereof shall be burnt up." It is necessary that this fire prepare men for the open day of eternity.

The day of time is seen and felt from the time the new-born infant has its eyes open, although it must be advanced in life to distinguish its light; so when the soul is brought forth to grace, it enjoys the beauty of it from the time its eyes are opened, but it cannot distinguish this light of grace until it has already advanced. All that is the temporal day, demanding neither death nor the consummation of the fire. But in order to enter into the eternal day, which is God Himself, the fire must consume everything, either upon the earth or in purgatory; and this is real and incontestable; for, in order that God may give Himself, and that we can enter into Him, there is necessary an all-divine purity taken in Himself, which absorbs and annihilates everything there is in the creature, either impure or of self, or straitened, which hinders what is purely divine in it from flowing into God. This, St. Paul calls an absorbent of everything mortal in us by life, in order that all mortality be swallowed up of life. So that grace as a created gift, however elevated it may be, causes not death; but God Himself, author of grace, eternal day, light of glory, source and essence of life, must necessarily cause death before receiving the soul into His eternal day, which is Himself.

> *31. But thou, remain here with me, and I will declare unto thee my commandments, my laws, and my ordinances, that thou mayest teach them to them, and that they may observe them in the land which I will give them for inheritance.*

There is another time when one can hear the voice of God without dying, and that is when one is already dead; as in heaven the blessed will see God, having been raised to die no more, and having been made like unto the angels. This is why Moses could speak to God and receive His oracles, and remain constantly near Him, having been dead and raised again mystically.

CHAPTER VI.

5. Thou shalt love the Lord thy God with all thy heart, with all thy soul, and with all thy strength.

God commands us to *love Him with all our heart;* meaning, to admit no affection, however holy and elevated it may be, neither of self, nor foreign, except for Him alone, and in Himself. So long as we do not love God above all interest whatsoever—whether virtue, salvation, or eternity—it is certain we cannot love Him with all our heart, since it is possible to love Him more. And who can doubt but that it is to love more generously, to love without any interest, than to seek in one's love something of self? Natural light alone teaches it to all, who believe themselves more beloved as they see no pretension to any advantage, but only a manifestation towards them of most disinterested good will. He, then, who loves God from interest, does not love Him *with all his heart,* although he loves Him from the heart, since he loves his self-interest along with God.

Whoever loves his own soul with God, and fears to lose it, who takes care of it, and loves to see it decorated with God's gifts, and enriched with great merits through self-affection, *does not love God with all his soul;* since he wishes still to take care of his soul in his divine loving, and he bends back on it a part of the love due entirely to God.

He who excepts something, and who does not lose everything for his God, does not love Him *with all his strength,* since he may love Him yet more strongly, abandoning himself fully to Him without any reserve. He who says, *with all his strength,* means a sovereign love, which goes as far as the capacity of the soul; and it must not be thought sufficient to sacrifice to God through a pure love one's temporal life and strength, if we do not also offer up our eternal life and strength.

Oh precept of PERFECT LOVE, hardly wilt thou be found accomplished under the heaven in all thy extent! And yet thou must be fulfilled in all thy perfection before entering into the paradise of heaven. This complete accomplishment is usually only found at the gate of heaven, after an entire purifying of the soul has given it birth, either in this life or in the other; and so soon as it is in this fullness and consummation out of this life, the entry of paradise must be opened to it, nothing now being able to retain a soul, which loves in this purity, from flowing for ever into God, who is truly become its God and its all, since He has become all its love.

6. These precepts which I give thee today shall dwell in thine heart.

It is no longer upon the stone that they are imprinted, it is too hard and too material to contain them. They must be *graven on the heart,* for it is only the heart that can receive this lesson. The language of love is learnt from love itself, and it is love that teaches love. Oh Love-God! It is Thou alone who can teach us to love Thee purely; it is Thou alone who teachest to the faithful souls the pure laws of Thy love, wholly exempt from all self-love, and which those that love themselves cannot understand. Truly, that is the law of the heart, known only by the heart, and not the law of stone, which, by reason of its resistance, cannot contain a law rendering the soul so supple and pliable to all God's will, whatever it be and whatever it cost; for the heart that loves, forgets all self-interest to think only of the friend. It is this law that tears away all our proper heart from itself to give it wholly to God, and that it may repose solely in Him ; this, earthly love has comprehended in its laws, saying, that the heart is more where it loves than where it beats. God has given Himself to man as a witness of His love for Him; and man abandons himself all to his God to give Him proofs of his love; and when this perfect state has been attained to, we can no more distinguish whether God is our heart, or our heart God.

15. For God is jealous, and the Lord your God is in the midst of you.

What? God is, *then, jealous* of man's heart? Yes; he wishes it entirely, and not a half. Jealousy cannot suffer a companion, were it even a king; God will have none, not even of the best things, and it is this jealousy that leads Him to strip the soul and to make it pass through so many strange states, so that, remaining divested of all natural good and supports, it may be void of everything, and be thus in a fit state to lodge the love of God. To love only for one's-self, the virtues, gifts, and favors of God is not to be worthy of Him. Oh! Is God not enough worthy to be loved to give Him all our heart, and great enough to occupy it entirely, without our wishing to retain something with Him.

It is in order that we may love Him with this sovereign love, and to guard Himself our heart, that He *dwells in the midst of us.* We must then be jealous for God, tearing from our heart without mercy all that would desire to lodge there with Him. Happy he who knows the generosity of the divine love! However great and beautiful things he thinks to know and publish of it, he will never know it if he does not experience it; and he only experiences it when it draws him out of himself to place him in God by the mystic transport, which can only be known by those in whom it is wrought, much surprised as they are to commence only then to discover the true disinterestedness and the pure generosity of love, which they believed they had comprehended for many years.

Whoever is placed in truth, knows and experiences God's jealousy so well that he allows himself to be proprietor of no good, however little; and if he did appropriate or retain to himself the least thing, Oh, with what horrible chastisement would this infidelity be punished! Those who have experienced the jealousy of a God could tell things of it that would make one tremble with fear; and the more He desires a heart for Himself, the more is He jealous of it. The Bridegroom is more jealous of His Bride than of His handmaidens, and when He admits a soul to His nuptial bed, O God, He suffers it to have nothing in the world, and tears all from it without mercy.

CHAPTER VII.

6. Ye are a holy people to the Lord your God, and the Lord your God has chosen you to be to him a peculiar people amongst all the peoples that are upon the earth.

This language of pure love and perfect charity is heard only by those who have advanced to an excellent degree of charity and naked faith; thus Scripture says that this people of love are *a holy people to the Lord.* This is a people holy for God and not for themselves, for they cannot wish the least holiness for themselves, nor any virtue. Were they to see themselves clad with anything appropriated to them, they would desire it to be quickly torn away, and would have the same horror of it as they would have of the devil.

O holiness, thou art only in God and for God! The sight of this truth will cause the saints, stripped of all other holiness, to see in heaven God's holiness alone, and will make them cry for ever, HOLY, HOLY, HOLY. For as in this abode of glory everything will be in pure and clear truth, all will be thus reduced into perfect unity; and this pure truth and perfect unity being only God Himself, holiness, which is composed of it, can be seen no more out of Him. And as all the blessed shall have received it from God alone, by Jesus Christ His Son, so will they all render it again most faithfully, and without power to preserve an atom thereof; to God alone by His Son. This St. Paul has expressed when he said, that *"Jesus* Christ must deliver up His kingdom into the hands of God and His Father, when He has put down all principality, all power, and all virtue; and when all things shall have been placed under His power, then the Son Himsclf shall be subject to Him, who has reduced everything under His feet, so that God may be all in all."

If a soul set on fire of this pure love were to see itself clothed with a holiness for itself, it would go, when placed in truth, to the depths of hell to be rid of it, having attained such a point that nothing is more insupportable to it than propriety, and it would rather accept anything else than suffer the least infection of it that it can recognize. It is on that account that this *people* is *holy to the Lord,* since being no longer proprietary, all their holiness is for God; and it is this that produces perfect charity, giving all to God, and taking away everything from the creature. But as this is rare, Scripture says, that this people of charity is the people *God has chosen to himself* (not for its graces, gifts, and favors), so that it may be to Him a *people peculiar* in love *above all the peoples of the earth.*

> 7. *The Lord has not joined himself to you, and has not chosen you, because ye were in greater num-*

ber than all the nations, since ye were of all the fewest in number.

8. But it is because he has loved you.

God *has not united himself* to His dear interior people, *because they are greater,* or more *numerous than other peoples;* since, on the contrary, they are the *smallest* in number, and the least in the opinion of men, on account of their stripping and annihilation, but He has united Himself to them *because He has loved them.* Yes, this people so small, so much a nothing in appearance, are loved by their God; and they are loved gratuitously by Him, without regard to their little merit. Is it not just that God should also be loved *by* them at the expense of everything?

9. Ye shall know that the Lord your God is mighty and faithful, keeping his covenant and mercy with those that love him and keep his commandments, to a thousand generations.

Scripture is admirable in its expressions. In order to show this soul which strips itself of all interest of salvation or holiness and of everything else, in order to love God purely, that God loves to see it lose everything for that, it assures this soul that its God, to whom it is abandoned, is *mighty and faithful;* mighty to draw it out of peril and to prevent it from falling, and too *faithful* to suffer it to be deceived when it abandons itself to Him without reserve, and hazards displeasing Him only to wish to please Him too much. Its love is not out of order, except that it loves beyond all rule; and God keeps His faithfulness even to the end with those that love Him.

CHAPTER VIII.

2. Thou shalt remember all the way by which the Lord thy God made thee pass through the wilderness for forty years, to afflict thee and try thee, to show what was in thy heart, and if thou wouldst keep his commandments or not.

How frightsome is the wilderness of faith, and how tiresome the length of its way! Moses brings to the *remembrance* of this people what happened to them at the end of this way, and tells them to forget it not, so that they may thus be confirmed in the assurance of their state. He desires them to *remember the road* they took, and how they were *afflicted and tried* for so long a time because God wished to see *what was in their heart,* as if He said, I wished to see if there remain anything in thine heart that could hinder My dwelling there. All these pains and abjections through which these souls pass are caused only for the purpose of emptying their heart, that God alone may refill it.

3. He has afflicted thee by famine, and given thee manna for food.

One of the greatest pains of the soul in this wilderness is *famine* and hunger, having been formerly so full and being here so empty. Were it given anything whereon to feed, even the most bitter in the world, it would find it sweet. It cannot be believed what this hunger of the soul caused by its self-love is: it destroys it and devours it, so that the pains are a relief to it, because they nourish it yet with something it feels, and which is a support to it. It is in this sense that Job said, that a soul thus enhungered finds bitter things sweet, and nourishes itself on food that once would have horrified it. God then *afflicts* these souls with this hunger in the wilderness of faith, but at the same time He *feeds* them *on manna,* which is so spiritual a food, that the soul finds therein nothing contenting it. This manna is a certain sustenance unknown and invisible which the soul does not distinguish on account of its purity; nevertheless, it is a sustenance which prevents it from perishing, for were it not supported (although imperceptibly) in so denuded states, it would quit everything.

> *3. Neither thy fathers, nor thou knewest this manna, but it was to teach thee that man does not live by bread alone, but by every word that proceedeth out of the mouth of God.*

It is certain that so long as the road of faith lasts, the soul *does not know of* the imperceptible support. The *fathers* even, however holy they were, had not known it so that they could speak of it, God not permitting it to be declared to souls; for if the greatness of this state could be made known to them, they would never allow themselves to be lost, nor would they ever come out of themselves. But if they have had some slight transient acquaintance with it, God takes away from them all the certitude of it by the most extreme reverses, so that they can lean upon it no longer. But, says Scripture, God makes the soul pass through these so terribly denuded states, *to make known to it that man does not live by bread alone,* namely, the gifts and perceptible graces serving for it as sensible and distinct sustenance; *but* that he lives much more *from God* Himself, which is signified by *every word that proceedeth out of His mouth.*

It must be remarked that it is not said simply by the word of God, which might be understood as to everything known and comprehended as of God; but *by every word proceeding out of His mouth.* Now this *speech which proceeds from his mouth* is His Word and Himself in essential unity, without means or medium of communication.

The *speech of God,* taken simply, is a mediate speech, received as a medium and in the faculties, by means of forms and images rendering it distinct and comprehensible; but the *word proceeding out of the mouth of God* is a substantial and immediate word issuing out of God Himself. The former is the word of God received out of Him, and the latter is the word of God dwelling in Himself; and which can only produce God.

In confirmation of all that I have advanced, Scripture does not say by every word that *has proceeded* out of the mouth of God,—for the word that has proceeded from God being out of Him, is a means and a created gift; but it expresses itself in the present tense, every word PROCEEDING out of the mouth of God, to show that it is this immediate word alone that is the word of God, and to mark by that the eternal and always real moment of the generation of the Word, who proceeds unceasingly out of the mouth of His Father, and who is never out of Him, as the Father says to Him always, "Thou art my Son, this day have I begotten Thee." God from all eternity begets His Word, and He begets Him unceasingly in all eternity by His immediate speech, which not being able to cease, finds in this Son its infinite termination equal to its principle, who is Speech-God; and this immediate speech proceeding from God and terminating in God, produces by a reflection of love between the Father who speaks, and the Son who proceeds from Him as speech, the Holy Spirit-God.

This could not be otherwise, since what has no other beginning than God, nor other termination than God, must necessarily be God: and it is clear that God producing it totally from Himself; as well as in everything equal to Himself, it is terminated in an immense God, who, by His infinity, receives as much as His Infinite principle can give Him. It must be, then, that this flux and reflux of all an immense and infinite God received into a God with the same qualities, should also produce a God of the same grandeur and immensity;

and as this Speech-God is wholly Himself; it must terminate in Him, for did it terminate out of Him, it would thus be annihilated, since He reserves to Himself nothing but what is communicated and given to His Word; so that everything is refound in the unity of essence, and it is this that forms the trinity of persons in the unity of the Divine Essence. A production of all God received wholly into God, and sent back again wholly to this same God, forms the ineffable mystery of the TRINITY. God interiorly sending (so to speak), and communicating totally, is called the Father: God receiving all God from God Himself, is called the Son, and of the reception of all God, and of the amorous regard of God communicating, and of God receiving and returning everything to the same God, proceeds God called the Holy Spirit. All this is veritably one same essence, and cannot be otherwise, being the same God communicating Himself, receiving, sending back, and proceeding.

This is found in the soul whom God favors with His immediate communications through its annihilation; taking no longer anything to itself of what God communicates to it, He communicates Himself to it: and by means of this same annihilation there being no longer anything mediate, God receives the return of His communication and after receiving it, He sends it back to Himself as pure as it issued forth; and it is this that produces the Holy Spirit, whence proceeds this perfect charity. For it must be known that God being immense and infinite, nothing can limit Him, and He fills all void by His immensity. Now, as He has nothing bounded or limited (and if He had anything finite He would not be God), there is also no void in which He does not perform this eternal generation of the Word; since if this was not the case, there would require to be a place which could contain God, or a void where the Word-God was not; which is equally absurd, since God would not then be infinite.

God then of necessity produces His Word in all creatures thus. But sin covers up and prevents the sight of these divine productions in such a manner that God forms them of necessity, and not with pleasure, in those rational creatures who have been infected by sin, and they do not at all perceive this mystery of eternity which is wrought in them, it being only revealed to the just souls in proportion as they become empty and annihilated, so that although God, even the Trinity, is in hell as well as in heaven, nevertheless He is there in a different manner, namely, He is present in hell out of the necessity of His essence which fills everything by its immensity, and not willingly from love and pleasure. But in these souls here spoken of God, forms these eternal productions as He pleaseth, without resistance on their part, and in a manner as agreeable as in the blessed, although they only know it by effects, and by lively and short illustrations which are given of them.

4. The rainment with which thou hast been clad has not been worn out by the length of time, nor have thy feet been hurt for these forty years.

It is surprising that although the soul passes through such strange states its *raiment is never worn out.* This raiment is *abandon* and the conduct of providence. *Abandon* serves it for a garment, and the more wretched it sees itself and the more God destroys it the more does it abandon itself to Him, without power to do otherwise. Now this *abandon* remains entire and *is not worn out,* although everything else perishes. The cloak is the conduct of providence, for the more a soul abandons itself the more does God take care of it, although often in a manner which, by covering it, loads it heavily: but no matter, whilst it remains in the way of faith, and does not issue out of it, these things *are never worn out* although they may be as old as ourselves, since they introduce the soul into the way and accompany it therein even to the end, without, during so long a road and time, either growing old or feeble.

Moses also observes to this people that *their feet have not been bruised,* for although they may often fall, yet for all that their feet are not hurt, unless they issue out of *abandon,* but as long as they remain abandoned and do not resume themselves whatever distress may happen to them, in spite of the weaknesses into which they fall in this frightful desert on account of its great nakedness, and although the senses, left to themselves, commit a thousand faults, caused by feebleness and surprise, yet all these hurt not the feet, for the affection of the soul is in no way harmed by them, it remains always firm and fixed in its God by an invariable and inviolable attachment, denoted by *the shoes* that are not worn out in the desert, and without being troubled at everything that takes *place outwardly.*

5. That thou mayest consider in thine heart that the Lord thy God has instructed thee, as a man teacheth his son.

God *instructs* these dear abandoned ones by their experience, *as a father instructs his son,* and *they consider in their heart* this excellent lesson when they have advanced, not knowing it by the lights of the spirit but by the inclination of the heart, and by the remembrance of experience, which remains so vividly imprinted in them that it leaves them no doubt of it. Man may indeed not know it whilst he is on the way, on account of the pain and incertitude of the road, but when he has arrived he cannot doubt but that the road by which he has walked is the true one, seeing that it has conducted him so straight, although across rocks and precipices and a thousand apparent perils, upon the brink of which he must walk without assurance of not falling therein, on the contrary, ready at every turn to fall, the darkness always enveloping this way.

6. And that thou mayest keep the commandments of the Lord thy God; to walk in his ways and to fear Him.

The soul is led thus to make it *walk,* without resistance, in the *will* of God, and to oblige it to obey Him with an inviolable fidelity although it may cost it something: and it is by this *abandon* to God's will, above all self interest, that it will be conducted to its end, which is God.

7. For the Lord thy God will bring thee into a goodly land, where there are brooks, quiet waters,

*and fountains, and where mighty rivers and depths
spring from its plains and hills.*

This is *a goodly land* since it is God who is
essential goodness. A land *where there are brooks,
quiet waters, and fountains,* since all sources are in
Him, and to be in God is to be in the source, but a
source of *rivers* by the abundance and impetuosity of
His communications, a source of *calm* and *tranquil
waters,* a source of useful *fountains,* agreeable and
refreshing. By these three kinds of waters Scripture
expresses all springing waters, to show that the soul
arrived in God through the emptiness and loss of all
good, and through the drying up of every other water
in this dry and arid desert, finds itself all filled with
these very waters, but in their spring and source, and
with the fullness of God Himself. Thus the soul, having lost all gifts and every grace, every facility of doing good, every acquired virtue, returning afterwards
to its end, finds everything in its very origin, not in
rivulets of communications, but in fullness of source;
and by losing everything for God alone, all is given
back to it in an eminent manner with God alone, since
the graces of God and all His greatness are with it—
not for the soul, which no longer takes anything of it,
but for God, being rich with His riches.

There are not only springs in God, but there are
bottomless *depths* and mighty *rivers,* of which something is shown to this soul. There are depths in which
it is lost never to come out; there, being contained in
the abyss itself, it is made one in it, and in this essential union there issues out from it (as from God, it

existing no longer, but God being in it and for it) rivers, waters, and fountains, to be distributed outwardly according to the need of every one. But it is necessary for this that it should have arrived not only at the land, God, - in which it lives and drinks as from the spring - but, moreover, it must be sunk, lost, transformed in God, in order that there may flow from God by it rivers, waters, and fountains; because these all *issue out of* the immense *plains* of the Divinity, *and from the mountains* of His power and grandeur.

> *8. A land of wheat, barley, and vines, of fig trees, pomegranates, and olives; a land of oil and honey.*

Scripture here particularises the Divine perfections which the soul possesses in God, and which are admirable fruits in Him. Goodness in man is of very little account; but in God, it is admirable. Charity out of God is insignificant, limited, and contracted; but in God, it is God Himself. In fine, all the good that we have lost for Him are found all gathered up and contained in Himself, as well as all the virtues, designated by all these kinds of fruits and trees, by the *oil* and *honey*.

> *9. Where thou wilt eat thy bread without any scarceness, and will enjoy abundance, of everything; a land whose stones are iron, and out of whose hills thou mayest dig brass.*

When the soul has attained to its origin, it *eats its bread without any poverty,* because everything that comes from God immediately, and all the virtues in God, being God, are deficient in nothing, but are all perfect; so that then it *enjoys* them without scarceness or defect. Not only that, but everything in it is useful; *the stone,* which out of it would be of no use, gives in it *iron* of the strongest and most necessary kind; and all metals and riches come out of its mountains: this is a confirmation of what has been said under diverse similitudes.

10. So that when thou hast eaten well and art full, thou mayest bless the Lord thy God for the excellent land which he has given thee.

Experience alone can make this known, therefore Moses said *when thou hast eaten,* that is to say experienced, *thou wilt be filled* with the fullness of God Himself, which fully satisfies the soul. Oh then *thou wilt bless the Lord thy God for the good land which he has given thee.*

14. Beware lest thy heart grow proud, and thou forget the Lord thy God who has brought thee out of Egypt and out of the house of bondage.

The only danger there can be in these states consists in souls coming to regard themselves full of so many riches, and attributing to themselves something of them, and delighting in it even to *forgetting* their former captivity and vileness. All this is to be feared for them: this sin alone caused the fall of the angel from heaven to hell, and it is this sin alone that can cause this soul to issue out of God and to be precipitated into hell. Therefore Moses is desirous that if this so advanced a people should be unfaithful enough to look upon their *elevation* in themselves that they should at the same time look upon their *former* captivity, out of which they never could have come had God not drawn them Himself, and by an effect of His absolute power.

> *15. It is he who led thee through this vast and terrible desert, where there were fiery serpents, scorpions, and vipers, where there was no water, and where he brought forth water out of the hard rock.*

He desires them also to remember how *it is he* alone who *led* them through so great and *terrible* a *wilderness,* full of *fiery serpents,* for the demons are all filled with fire and fury to destroy the souls that are in this desert. They journey the whole length of this road, surrounded by sins and the rage of their enemy, how then could they have come out of it if God had not brought them? So much the more, as this wilderness was so dry that *there was not* a drop of *water* other than what God *brought forth out of the* hard *rock:* this water which is found in so great a desert is the hardness and insensibility of naked faith which does not permit this soul to think of so many perils, nor to recognize them such as they are, being immovable as the rock is in defending itself, but this water which serves it for sustenance amongst inevitable dangers is given only by God, since it is He alone who not only delivers from perils and from all enemies, but it is also He who imparts to the souls this advantageous firmness so that it may neither be stung nor terrified.

> *16. Who fed thee in the wilderness with manna, which thy fathers knew not, and who, after hav-*

*ing afflicted and tried thee, had pity upon thee at
the latter end.*

All this really takes place in this manner and in
the same order. After God has tried the soul by all the
demons, miseries, and sins, and by all its enemies represented by these venomous beasts, and whilst all this
time it has been deprived of all succour of sensible,
distinct, and perceptible graces, of all refreshment and
nourishment, having only for support the water of its
firmness and insensibility, which appears to it a final
reprobation and impenitence, He *gives to it* also
manna, which is a secret and hidden support and not
apparent to it, but by which God prevents it from wholly
perishing. He feeds it also upon His sacred body, which
however gives it no consolation, although it sustains
it: on the contrary, the soul thinks it entirely profanes
it, and would rather be deprived of it, so that the nakedness and distaste which it finds in this kind of nourishment augment its pain the more. But although this
appears thus to the interior senses and faculties, nevertheless the divine sacrament yet continues to be a
great sustenance, although wholly spiritual, unknown,
and concealed from the soul.

After, I say, all these trials, God comes Himself to *afflict* this soul and to lay His heavy hand upon
it. Oh the terrible affliction of this! It is beyond all
expression. *Let God come himself to combat a leaf
which the least wind driveth to and fro* (Job xiii. *25).*
Ah! This is what cannot be expressed. Often this rash
leaf thinking to do well, and not imagining that it is
Himself, the Strong Armed, wishes to defend itself

and these defenses serve only to cause it inexplicable griefs. This poor leaf must then at last bend, yield, and fall to the ground, and be in fine consumed by God Himself. All the other trials which preceded were nothing to this one; for God who sustained this soul in an unknown and imperceptible manner, repelled the burning darts of the demons, the stings and bites of sin, and having rendered the soul very firm and insensible, these merely grazed it, or at most terrified it without doing it any hurt: but this other *trial* of which I speak can come neither from nature nor demons; it must be God alone, who mercilessly causes this rock to bend like a leaf; overturns it, and in fine annihilates and consumes it, and it is solely the operation of God. Serpents may, by their envenomed wounds, cause death, but it is only God who has the power to destroy, consume, and annihilate this soul in His vast bosom, and in fine transform it in Himself.

This operation, being the most subtle and powerful of all, is the least sensible, because it is neither in the interior senses nor in the faculties, but in the most profound center and supreme part of the soul. It is only God who can perform it, and He does it by causing the center to suffer, purging it radically from all propriety and dissimilarity, in order, by annihilating it, to lose it into Himself, which causes this operation, although the most insensible of all, to be nevertheless the heaviest. But God, after having thus *afflicted* this soul, and having overwhelmed it with His own weight, after having destroyed and consumed it, *consoles it at the end,* which means that He only consoles it when it after having destroyed and consumed it, *consoles it at the end,* which means that He only consoles it when it is in its end, which is Himself. And when the soul has arrived there it knows that what appeared to it formerly a rigorous justice was a great *mercy.*

> *17. That thou mayest not say in thine heart, It is my power and the might of my hand that hath gotten me all these great riches.*

> *18. But that thou mayest remember the Lord thy God, and that it is he who has given thee this power to fulfill his covenant.*

There is nothing in Scripture which does not express and confirm all this. It is, it says, that thou mayest not attribute any power to thyself that God destroys thee thus, and that thou mayest not say, *it is my hand that hath done* all this, that is to say, I have *acquired these great riches* by my labor, my cares, and my fidelity, *but that thou mayest remember* that all strength lies in God and all weakness in thyself, and that it is He alone who has performed this great work. Thus such a soul is far removed from attributing anything to itself, God enclosing so great things in earthen vessels, that the power may be attributed to Him, and not to man, who seeing only his own earth and vileness cannot appropriate to himself anything.

CHAPTER IX.

1. Hear me, Oh Israel! Thou wilt pass this day over Jordan, and wilt find a people stronger than thou.

3. But the Lord thy God will pass before thee as a burning and devouring fire to destroy them.

This passage of Jordan signifies the issuing out of the soul from itself to be received into God. It must pass through its enemies. God goes before as a *devouring fire to destroy* and consume all their strength.

4. But when the Lord thy God shall have destroyed them before thee, say not in thine heart, Because of my righteousness the Lord hath brought me into this land to possess it, and these nations have been cut off for their wickedness.

The thought that offends God the most of all, consists in the soul beginning to believe or imagine that *it is because of its* innocence and fidelity *that God has performed* on its behalf so many wonders, and that *the others* have been deprived of them on account of their sins. Ah! God has no regard for our self-*righteousness* to do us so many great mercies, since His end is to destroy our self-righteousness. But it is necessary that the soul remain fixed without regarding itself, viewing everything in the power of God and nothing in itself, without examining anything; for all self-righteousness must be destroyed in order to attain to this point. It is not then for our righteousness that we arrive at it, and God destroys in us all self-righteousness only that we might not believe that it could give us entrance into Him.

> *5. For it will not be for thy good works, nor for the uprightness of thy heart that thou wilt enter into the land to possess it.*

Moses seems by all these repetitions not to be able to show too often that no *work,* no *uprightness,* nor any self-righteousness can procure so great a good. For if anything can obtain it it would be, more than anything else, *uprightness* and integrity, but even this perishes, and God as Himself cannot be possessed by any good, nor by any intermediate means.

> *6. Know then that it is not for thy righteousness that the Lord thy God has put thee in possession of this good land, since thou art a stiff-necked people.*

> *7. But remember, and never forget how thou hast provoked the anger of the Lord thy God in the wilderness, and how thou hast always been rebels*

against the Lord from the day when thou didst depart out of Egypt until now.

He again shows them, and recommends them most particularly *not to forget* that they have not ceased to sin and to *provoke the wrath of God* from the time when He brought them out of the active state. And in the remainder of this chapter he represents to them in detail all the sins they committed on the long road of the wilderness.

Oh wisdom, oh profundity of the word of God! The sight of our sins and of our infidelities without number, ought indeed to persuade us that it is not through our own merits that He has chosen us for interior states, and for the purity of His love, the more as, since He has penetrated us with His liveliest lights, and gratified us with the mystic ray, we have not ceased to be ungrateful and rebellious against Him. God acts thus, then, before making the soul enter into Himself: He shows it in detail all its infidelities and offences, which overthrows it, and casts it even into the abyss.

At the end (v. 26) Moses concludes by confessing for God's glory alone, that He has acted thus with so much goodness towards His people, because they are His, and are *His inheritance,* and He has *redeemed* and conducted them by His *mighty power and outstretched arm,* that is to say, because He has chosen them gratuitously, to signalize on their behalf His power, His wisdom, and His love.

*9. The tribe of Levi has had no part nor inherit-
ance with his brethren, for the Lord himself is his
portion, as the Lord thy God hath promised him.*

To be *the inheritance of God;* is to be given up
to Him, and to be conducted by Himself, as was this
abandoned people; but *to have God for our inheritance,* can only take place when the soul is entirely annihilated. Therefore, these souls wholly confirmed and
annihilated, *have no part* in the sensible graces or perceptible goods of the others, *God* alone being *their
portion,* and their hereditary portion, as David, that
great mystic, experienced, when he sung with truth,
*Oh God, thou art the God of my heart, and my por-
tion forever."* This is also what has been experienced
in a peculiar manner by the family of Levi, the family
of high priests and annihilated ones.

*14. Behold the heaven, and the heaven of heav-
ens is the Lord thy God's, the earth also, and all
that it contains.*

By the *heaven* is meant the faculties elevated
and united to God; and by *the heaven of heavens* is
signified the center where God dwells. He says, then,
that not only is the union formed in the faculties, and
that they are God's, but that the center also, the heaven
of heavens, belongs to Him by essential union. For as
man's spirit is well called his heaven, so the supreme
part of the spirit is very well denominated the heaven
of heavens; and the word *behold* expresses that it is a
state already arrived.

17. The Lord thy God is the God of gods, and the Lord of lords, the Great God; mighty and terrible, who regardeth not persons, nor taketh reward.

As the heaven of heavens is God's, it is there also where *the God of gods* dwells as in his lofty Zion, which is reserved for Him. This well expresses that it is not only God's graces that dwell there, and which are often taken for God Himself; but it is the God of gods, the God of all that, and the author of all these sacred gifts, who dwells in the heaven of heavens. He adds that it is *the Lord of lords* Himself, *this Great God,* strong, *mighty, terrible,* such as He is in Himself. But this God, who giveth Himself entirely, *regardeth not persons* nor gifts; everything personal and proper must be destroyed and annihilated; likewise also must we be emptied and cleared of all his gifts; then it is that God receives into Him the nothing, but were it not so, it would never be received there.

21. He is thy praise and thy God, who has done these wonders and marvels which thine eyes have seen.

God Himself has become the *praise* of this soul: He praises Himself in it, and it has no other praise than Himself, who, after having performed *great* and terrible things in it, becomes in fine its praise, as to Him alone all the praise is due: and *its eyes behold it all,* full knowledge of it being given it.

CHAPTER XI.

10. The land whither thou goest to possess it, is not like the land of Egypt, from whence thou comest, where after sowing the seed, waters are brought to water it as a garden.

11.But there are mountains and plains which drink in the rain of heaven.

12. And the Lord thy God careth for it continually, and his eyes watch over it, from the beginning of the year till the end.

This difference between the *lands of Egypt* and the promised land is admirable: the former, representing the multiplied state, need to be *watered like gardens,* and this watering is no other than this good activity, without which these lands would produce nothing; but not so with the latter. *There are* souls elevated like *mountains,* others agreeable and fertile like *plains,* but both being perfectly passive, labor not to water; they drink in only *the rains of heaven,* not being watered by earthly waters, but by heavenly ones. And God unceasingly *looks upon* this land without abandoning it for a moment, and *his eyes are upon it from the beginning even to the end,* without ceasing for one instant to regard it.

Oh happiness of a soul which, in the cessation from all self labor, remains exposed and in waiting to receive the rain of heaven! Such a soul is never confounded in its expectation, for God is never a moment without guarding it by the care of His providence; He *watches* for it when it rests. Is not the work of a God preferable to that of the creature? Abandon, abandon, and leave God to act!

13. If then thou observest the commandments that I give thee today, thou wilt love the Lord thy God, and thou wilt serve him with all thy heart, and with all thy soul.

All the graces and commandments which God gives us tend only to cause Him to be *loved with the whole heart,* because of the jealousy He entertains for this heart, which lie desires all for Himself. He asks only love. Oh, pure love, how rare thou art! Thou costest all the cares and labors of a God; thou costest all the sufferings and frightful strippings of the creature! Oh pure love, where art thou to be found? In God alone, and thou canst not be in the soul unless God alone be there. Thou art in Him, thou issuest from Him, and thou returnest into Him; but out of Himself, considered as the principal, center, and termination of this love, there is nothing but impurity.

Chapter XII.

8. Ye shall not act then as we do here this day, every man doing that which seemeth right in his own eyes.

Moses means that these dear abandoned ones when they have arrived at the promised land will no longer there do the same things as in the desert of faith, nor as fruits of their own uprightness, nor with difficulty or restraint, for having attained to a divine state, which is a state of innocence, they will do all that is *just,* no longer because it *seems to them* such, nor by reason of their own righteousness, but because they shall then be moved by the righteousness of God Himself, and they will thus act in entire freedom; for although they are to perform more things in the promised land than they did in the desert, as Moses declares to them by the enumeration which he makes in this chapter, nevertheless they will perform them in unity and repose, as God does all things, for they will perform in God and by the gentle impulse of the law of His love, which although multiplied in its effects is perfectly united and peaceful in its principle.

He has told them before that it was not for their righteousness that they would be introduced into this land, for this righteousness being proper to them was not pure enough to enter therein; but the righteousness which is to bring them into it is the righteousness of God Himself, which is exempt from all deceit, for the soul having been placed in truth, which is the eternal law (just as the people of Israel were ruled by the law of God given by Moses), it can judge of things only as God judges of them; thus all that is right in the eyes of God is right in its eyes, which now see things only with God's eyes; this is the cause of its being free from mistakes and of its living in full liberty, although men think otherwise of it.

9. For ye are not as yet entered into the rest and inheritance which the Lord your God will give you.

The reason why they have not as yet received this freedom and divine righteousness is that they have not yet arrived *at the rest and inheritance of the Lord;* but when they shall have *entered* therein, oh then they will find nothing that can straiten them, everything being done with an admirable freedom and the greatest purity, because everything is done in God.

10. That ye may enjoy a perfect rest in the midst of all the enemies that surround you, and dwell there without fear.

12. There shall ye eat and rejoice in the presence of the Lord your God, ye and your sons, your daughters, your men-servants and your maid-ser-

226

vants, and the Levite that dwelleth in your cities,
for he hath no part nor inheritance amongst you.

There they will possess great peace even *in the midst of all their enemies,* who will not dare to come near them. Then *they will dwell without fear,* being, as it were, placed in a permanent state. They will be *in* a joy and freedom wholly innocent, and their rejoicings will be made before God: *the sons and daughters, men-servants and maid-servants* will all have part in this joy of innocence; *the Levites* also, who are the most eminent persons and the leaders of others, *and who dwell in the same cities* with them, will share in this pleasure; and this joy they will have in common with you, since it is the only thing that remains to them, to share with you. David had experienced that when he said, "All they that are in thee, O Lord! are as persons ravished with joy."

> *17. Thou mayest not eat within thy cities the tithe of thy corn, of thy wine, and of thy oil.*
>
> *18. But thou shalt eat them before the Lord thy God in the place which the Lord thy God shall choose, thou, and thy sons and thy daughters, thy men-servants and thy maid-servants, and the Levite who dwelleth with you; thou shalt refresh thyself and be filled before the Lord thy God, in all the works of thy hands.*

How many things are there *not permitted in the cities,* that is to say, in the presence of men, which one can nevertheless do innocently before God: St. Paul has well experienced it, (i Cor. ix. and x.) It is in this sense that Moses says, *thou shalt not eat the tithes within thy cities;* by this word *thy* is meant the souls that are still in possession of themselves, and by *cities* those persons that are offended: the *tithes* denote lawful observances, which are all united in love. How many things would appear hurtful to feeble and unenlightened souls, and would offend them, which nevertheless are in truth but the purest manner of fulfilling the *law!*

But this is only known to souls of this degree who are divinely enlightened. We must render ourselves weak with the weak in order not to offend them. All things are lawful to Paul, but all things are not expedient; all things are permitted to an Apostle, but all things do not edify.

It is necessary also that these tithes be eaten *with joy, and in the place which God has chosen;* it is He who does all things, who gives certain laws to the soul and delivers it from them; and this rejoicing will be universal, extending to the superior part signified by *the Levite,* and to the inferior denoted by the male and female *servants.* In fine, we must *be filled* with the goods of the Lord, *and be refreshed in everything that we do,* acting with a holy freedom which God Himself gives, free from returnings or vexations.

> *20. When the Lord thy God shall have enlarged thy border, as he has promised thee, and thou shalt have desired to eat flesh according to thy longing.*

God, having enlarged and greatly *extended* the soul, places it in a new liberty, by which it may *eat* with safety what previously would have caused its death. In the wilderness the people were punished in a terrible manner for desiring *flesh,* and here they are permitted to eat of it as much as they desire, without any evil happening to them; on the contrary, they are exhorted to do so with joy, and in the presence of the Lord. Oh! Scripture decides it, when it says that the first time they *lusted* after it, (Numbers xi. 34); therefore the place of their punishment was called the tomb of concupiscence: but here they are very far removed from eating it in this manner; they eat it only because it is permitted and ordained to them; they eat it to do the will of God and not to satisfy their sensuality; thus they eat it with joy, all lust and malignity having been taken away from them. These souls can no longer think of mortifying themselves, but they make use of everything innocently and without scruple in the name of God. "Let him that eateth of all things not despise him that eateth not, and let him that maketh a scruple to eat not condemn him that eateth" (Rom. XIV. 3); for the Lord has numbered him amongst His own, amongst the number of those who, being perfectly His, find His good pleasure in all things.

CHAPTER XIV.

1. Be ye the children of the Lord your God. Ye shall not cut yourselves, nor shave yourselves, on account of the death of your friends.

2. For ye are a people holy unto the Lord your God, and whom he hath chosen from all the nations that are upon the earth to be unto him a peculiar people.

Moses commands this people to be like little *children.* This is the character of these innocent souls, to be without malice. He forbids them at the same time to wound or *cut* themselves, for children do not these things, but they live from Providence, receiving what happens to them, and seeking nothing. The reason why he gives them these commands is, because they are *people holy unto the Lord their God;* as if he said to them, not being holy for yourselves, you have nothing to do with these marks of affected holiness; but being holy *for God,* ye must be holy as He desires, that is, be children, since He declares that this is what He loves the most, and it is that you might become children that *he has chosen you from all the nations of the earth to be his peculiar people.*

CHAPTER XXVII.

18. The Lord hath chosen you this day to be unto him a peculiar people.

19. And to raise you above all the nations which he hath made for his praise, for his glory, and for the grandeur of his name; that ye may be the holy people of the Lord your God, as he hath spoken.

He *raises this people today,* that is to say, in His eternal day, as has been explained above, that they may be *peculiar to himself* alone; therefore He renders them more excellent than any other, and *than all the nations which he hath made for his praise, for his glory, and for the grandeur of his name.* All the other good and holy ways are made for the praise of God, and people labor therein for His glory and to bless His holy name; but His praise, His name, and His glory are less than Himself; and are not Himself in that they are out of Him. But these annihilated souls, without thinking either of praise or of glory, are *the holy people of the Lord,* for they have lost all things in order to render to Him a perfect homage to His holiness by their lowliness and misery, to His strength by their weaknesses, to His justice by the loss of their own self-righteousness. The others render glory to God by praising Him with all their might; but these are the saints of God through their own destruction, for all self-holiness is lost in them, in order that the holiness of God may alone exist there. They are not holy for men who know them not; they are not holy for themselves, believing themselves full of sin, and sin itself. They are not holy for praise, honor, and glory, nor for any of those things which appear of some note, since far from that, they possess only abjection, contempt, and confusion for their lot.

CHAPTER XXVII.

9. Hearken diligently, Oh Israel, this day art thou made the people of the Lord thy God.

It is only at the moment of the going out from ourselves, that we are truly *made a people to the Lord,* although until then we may have been always consecrated to Him by the life of His grace; since it is in this *day* that the soul, losing all propriety, finds itself disposed to be received into God. It becomes also peculiarly His people in that, having gone out from itself it resists Him no longer; for every soul resists God just as much as it remains in itself, and it becomes to Him so much the more supple the more it comes out.

CHAPTER XXVIII

9. The Lord shall in thee establish a holy people to himself if thou keep the commandments of the Lord thy God and walk in his ways.

Not only will they be a *people* to the Lord by transient disposition, but they will be *established* in this state; and it will be *for himself* that God will render them firm in His *holiness,* if they do His will and are faithful to *walk in his ways.*

12. The Lord will open unto thee the heaven as his richest treasure.

To open the heaven as his richest treasure is to give communication of all that is in the heaven, as much the possession of Himself as the knowledge given only in heaven, or to souls who have attained to this state.

15. But if thou obey not the voice of the Lord thy God,

19. Thou shalt be cursed in thy comings in and in thy goings out.

But he that quits so beautiful a way, and who, by a frightful infidelity, goes out from his God, *shall be cursed* from that moment *in returning* into his propriety; and cursed in his going out, by withdrawing himself from his God by a calamity similar, in some respects, to that of Lucifer.

> *20. He shall smite thee with famine and with want; he shall break and consume thee on account of thine own inventions, by which thou hast withdrawn thyself from him.*
>
> *21. He shall add thereto the scourge of the pestilence.*
>
> *23. The heaven shall be as brass above thee, and the earth under thy feet shall become as iron.*
>
> *25. The Lord will suffer thee to fall before thine enemies.*
>
> *26. And thy dead body shall be the prey of all the birds of the heaven.*
>
> *28. He shall strike thee with madness, with blindness, and with frenzy of heart.*

Thou shalt then be overwhelmed by all the evils possible, being, as it were, in a hell in which sin and the demon will take vengeance upon thee; sin will cling to thee like *the pestilence,* and all the other woes will follow, so that thou shalt be delivered up to all *thine enemies;* thou shalt suffer all the evils of guilt and punishment which will fall upon thee. *The heaven will become as brass for thee,* no longer being willing to hear thee; so that thou wilt scarcely be able any longer to pray or be converted. Oh woe! woe! In place of the dew of grace, there is nothing now but dust. Then these souls *fall before all their enemies,* who kill them by mortal sin. Everything comes little by little, and from bad to worse. What were only wounds become *deaths,* for afterwards there come *blindness* and obduracy in this state, and also *madness of heart,* which is despair.

CHAPTER XXIX.

4. The Lord hath not given you until this day a
heart to know, nor eyes to see, nor ears to hear.

It is true that although one walks in the way,
one cannot *know* all these things, nor be *enlightened*
as to them or *comprehend* them, until one has arrived
at the termination. All that might have been said regarding them previously, could not be comprehended
by the person while he was on the *way;* but he has no
sooner arrived than he is astonished to see how his
eyes are opened, how his *heart* perceives, and how he
has an understanding of all things.

26. God will cast those out of the land who serve
strange gods.

28. He will drive them out in his wrath and fury,
and in his extreme indignation, sending them into
a strange land.

By these are meant those who have resumed
themselves, and becoming again proprietary, will have
withdrawn themselves by their wickedness from the

241

dominion of God, to conduct themselves in their own ways; and who, preferring self-interest to *abandon,* will have quitted the place of repose to return to the care of themselves. These will, from that moment, be *cast out by God in his wrath, and sent into a strange land,* into a place where there will be no more rest for them.

CHAPTER XXX.

2. If thou return to the Lord, and if thou obey all his commandments, with all thy heart and soul, as I command thee this day, and also thy children,

3. The Lord thy God will bring thee again from the place of thy captivity; He will have compassion on thee, and will gather thee together again from all the places whither thou wast before scattered.

Moses, however, affirms that if these criminal and rejected souls begin to *return towards God, and to obey him with all their heart,* He will draw them out of their captivity. If these persons are with difficulty converted, it does not arise on the part of my God, who being all love and mercy, "wills not the death of the sinner, but rather that he should turn and live." I say again that the difficulty of their conversion comes not from the part of God, who holds always His arms open to receive those who are willing to return to Him; and as, says St. Augustine, when we cast ourselves into His arms, we must not think that He withdraws them and suffers us to fall. Oh no, it would be impious to think so, for it was for that that He died with His arms extended upon the cross; but this difficulty proceeds from the soul, which being established in a state of consistence, can only be moved with great difficulty. Moreover, having been for a long time in a state of inability to distinguish itself from God, on account of its intimate union, it cannot, in any way, either turn itself away from God, nor return to Him; and through long usage, it can scarcely now change its conduct, although it has really fallen.

This is then, what renders these sorts of falls and repentances equally so difficult, namely, this establishment and state of consistence in God which makes the heart scarcely pliable either on one side or another.

And the soul can only issue out of it in two ways; either by the pride of Lucifer, which leads it to attribute to itself the power and might of God, taking complacency in its state, and regarding itself vainly, whence it is carried away even to attributing to its own strength or merits what God does in it and by it. And as these unfaithful persons imitate the evil angels in their fall, having fallen from so eminent a degree of grace and holiness, they imitate them also in their impenitence, their conversion being rendered so much the more difficult, as they have sinned with the more ingratitude and the less feebleness.

The other manner of going out from God is by resuming one's self, and voluntarily withdrawing one's self from His dominion in order to re-enter into one's own conduct, and becoming thus proprietary. Behold, then, the two kinds of sins by which these souls commence their disaster; the wandering of the mind by pride and vain complacency, and the wandering of the will, rendering one's self proprietary, and withdrawing from the dominion of God. This is then the source of all the other sins they commit afterwards. It thus may be easy to see that it is most difficult for them to do this voluntarily and to be lost. This is why there are few or no examples of souls arrived at this point who have fallen; but it is sufficient that it may happen, for us to be on our guard.

What then causes these souls to have so much difficulty in returning to God after their fall, comes from their being established in a state of consistence, and remaining content in the evil as they were rendered firm in the good. And this is also what has caused the impossibility of Lucifer's conversion. They can no longer turn themselves towards God, on account of the unity which they had with Him, and through which they have lost the habit of turning. But what renders the thing almost impossible is this, that these persons desire to perform their repentance from the active side, as formerly, and those who conduct them desire it also, which is as impossible as it is useless. It is necessary then, O directors, that without tormenting such souls as these with active penitence, you make them enter solely into a sight of their own humiliation, as far as they are capable of it, leaving them to drink deep draughts of the wrath and indignation of God; teaching them to remain submitted to His divine justice, content never to be pardoned if such be His will, without distressing themselves as to whether they will be pardoned and re-established in grace or not. Since they have fallen from so high a degree, and have lost so many graces, it is necessary that, stripped of all self-interest, they should remain exposed thus to the extremist blows of divine justice. They must not make any effort to return to a lower manner of prayer than that to which they had attained at the time of their fall, not even although the directors exact it of them; for it is just as impossible as to make a man re-enter his mother's womb, and besides the fact that they would never succeed in it, they would, moreover, by it be hindered from advancing. Retaining them then in their degree, O fathers of these souls, abandon them without mercy to divine justice, permitting them not the slightest deliverance or departure from it. O frightful repentance, and how few have the courage to abandon themselves to it; and even how few directors have the courage to leave to it those souls who have been committed to them! This is what has caused so much devastation in the spiritual life after the falls, for want of applying the suitable remedies. People are offended with the feeble ones, and despair of the poor fallen ones. But if souls were faithful and courageous enough to suffer themselves to be burned and consumed by divine justice, they would, in a short time, be re-established in a state perhaps more elevated than that from which they had fallen, as God promises by His prophet, for the consolation of this kind of penitent ones—" I have turned my face from thee for a moment in the time of my wrath, but I have looked upon thee afterwards with a never-ending mercy."

The reasons why this sort of repentance is the proper one for souls advanced in the passive way, are (besides what has been already advanced), firstly, that nothingness is the immediate disposition for the supernatural, the fullness of God being distributed only into the emptiness of the creature. Now persons thus fallen from a high degree, having been in an eminent supernatural state, and who are to be again re-established therein, need for that the most supernatural communications, and consequently must remain in nothingness through the acceptation and love of their abjection, and by their eternal abandonment to the disposition of God, in order to be in a state to receive them; otherwise, wishing to fill themselves anew with practices and self-inventions and efforts, they would thus place a new obstacle to the richest graces necessary to raise them and make them enter anew into their degree, just as any form gains admittance more easily into a subject empty and bare than into another where there is something to empty or purify.

Secondly, it is certain that the more the soul renounces its own interests to sacrifice itself to those of God, so much the more is it disposed to a more speedy and advantageous conversion, for nothing touches God's heart more, leading Him to show great mercy, than to see His poor creature rather accept all the blows of His justice than retain any self interest, or not sacrifice itself unreservedly to His glory; and even from the time when it is really in this disposition it is perfectly converted, it being impossible for sin to exist with so heroic a charity, and that grace should not be found in a heart burning with so pure a love that it accepts all that can be accepted for the interests of God throughout the whole extent of His will, justice, and power. As this then is infallibly the speediest and most perfect conversion, and as moreover this soul is capable of it, seeing that these are fruits of the state from which it has fallen, and it has still a facility and kind of habit of performing these renouncements and sacrifices so intensified, it is necessary to conduct it by this way, and to teach it not only to abandon itself entirely to God, who alone can apply the needful remedy for its ill and show His glory thereby, but also not even to desire this remedy, preferring the good pleasure of God to the cure of its mortal wound. This is then the most sovereign remedy for so great an evil, nothing being in anything more sure, nor more in order than when it is left the most fully to God.

Persons who read this will perhaps think that this penitence is not conformable to the fall; and that it is not a pain and grief, and does not afflict the soul. But if they had the experience of it they would confess that nothing in the world equals this pain. It is the purest purgatory, or even hell, according to the degree in which God places them, and which is an inexplicable torment. Oh how much more skilful God is in purifying than any creature, and how very different the punishments of an avenging God are from all the inventions of the justice of men! Such a soul would rather suffer all possible torments than remain as we have said, (faithful and without stirring) under the hand of divine justice. All the penances that it could be made to do, even the most extreme, would solace it and form a refreshment for it.

It is necessary well to guard against allowing these things to be done to it, for this would draw it still further from its state, and would prevent it from being reestablished therein. It is natural that one should rise where one falls, and thence continue one's way, without wishing to return to the beginning in order to rise, or retrace all the road because one has fallen before finishing it. Moreover it would not be a penance for this soul to burden it with mortifications, this would rather be a refreshment. This is easy to conceive. The pain of austerities and outward penances afflicts the senses but consoles the spirit; now as in these souls the senses are in a great measure dead, as much because that having exhausted all the penances and mortifications possible for them, they have become almost insensible to them, as because the senses being separated from the spirit have no more vigour, so that they scarcely feel pleasures and pains; it is no longer by the senses that their penitence must be measured, but that the punishment may be more grievous for them, and also proportionate to their fault, it must be a punishment of the spirit, all their sin being of the spirit.

Now in order that this pain of spirit may be lively, profound, and equal to the fault, it can be inflicted only by God Himself. Whatever, then, is done to the senses, would be an amusement and support for the spirit, diverting it from its pain. But when the spirit finds itself overwhelmed under the weight of divine justice, and senses, which solace it in nothing, ah! This is a frightful torment, and such as experience alone can make understood. It is a fire penetrating even to the marrow by its activity, and I affirm that of a thousand persons who have fallen, there will not perhaps be found three willing to suffer themselves to be devoured by justice, in all its extent, without resuming themselves sooner or later; above all in sickness, or near death, for then one desires to make all sorts of efforts to be assured of salvation by self-activity.

But it is certain that it is not necessary for these souls to do more at death than at another time; on the contrary, it is at this time that one must abandon one's-self, with more courage, to divine justice, to bear even its weight through all eternity. Oh! That is the purity of disinterested love, unknown by self-love, but known, esteemed, embraced by pure love! A person happy enough to die thus would render to God an ineffable glory; and without passing through any purgatory (for what can there remain to purge in a soul possessing nor more propriety, and arrived at so heroic a charity?) would be elevated to the highest degree in the heavens; in the place of which, when people resume themselves at death, they cause God to lose a very great glory, and they lose also an eminent happiness; not that the person is not saved, but he must, in the other life, finish the payment of his cowardice,

This is of more consequence than it is possible to tell, and I pray that those persons into whose hands these writings may fall, will give particular attention to it.

4. Although thou shouldst have been driven to the pole of heaven, from thence will the Lord thy God bring thee;

5. And he will take thee again and bring thee into the land which thy fathers possessed; and he will bless thee, so that thou shalt be multiplied greater than thy fathers.

Should a soul be happy enough to enter into the disposition which we have just named, although it had been rejected of God, and removed from Him, by the enormity and long duration of its fall, as far as the *poles* are distant from one another, He would again call it back and reunite it to Himself. He would even give it a more ample *blessing,* and a grace more abundant than what it had before its fall, because of the purity of the love with which it had acted towards Him.

6. The Lord thy God will circumcise thy heart, and the heart of thy children, that thou mayest love the Lord thy God with all thy heart, and with all thy soul, and that thou mayest live.

God Himself *will cut off from this heart* all that had contributed to its fall, so that this person *may love* Him always *with all his heart* without resuming himself any more, and *may live again* in Him for ever, with a life more abundant, considering the degree in which he was before his fall.

9. The Lord shall return to resume in thee his delights amongst so many goods, as he rejoiced in thy fathers.

He *takes his pleasure* in this soul that has returned to Him, and dwells there with *delight,* because it is more exempt from self-love than ever, and its fall has been to it the occasion of having still greater estrangement from, and hatred of; itself; and also more confidence in and love for God.

11. This commandment which I make unto thee this day, is not above thee, nor far removed from thy knowledge.

This way is not, as almost every one thinks, a thing so *difficult* or *distant;* that is, so rare, and extending to so few persons. All are capable of it, since for this it is only necessary to have a heart well submitted to God, and the principal part of the work depends on His grace, which is equally powerful to perform it in all those perfectly abandoned to it, and faithful to allow themselves to be pursued, destroyed, and annihilated. But the cause of so few souls being desirous of entering therein is self-love, which leads souls to regard themselves, and to resume themselves, to take care of themselves, and to fear to abandon themselves to God, thinking they do better conducting themselves than in blindly trusting themselves to God.

12. It is not in the heaven that thou shouldst say, who among us can mount up to heaven to bring it unto us?

Almost all excuse themselves in this manner from entering the way of faith. This is *too high* for us, they say, it is only good for the heavenly souls. Moses knowing well that this would be the most dangerous temptation, for it is covered with the veil of humility distinctly warns them of it. For all persons who are at a distance from so great a good, think they are perfectly right when they say, 'we are not worthy of it, we dare not aspire to it, it would be a presumption.' I say, however, that this is not the true humility, but pusillanimity; and that if it were true that these souls could have all the advantages of the others without risking anything, oh with what open heart would they not receive them! It is not the graces that they flee, nor the merits and crowns dependent on them, but it is that there are pains and incertitudes to be borne in order to attain to them, along with the stripping of sensible and luminous gifts, which they fear to lose.

Moreover, it will be acknowledged that all persons who practice the humility-virtue, are far removed from the humility which causes annihilation. By the humility-virtue the more you think you abase yourselves, the more you make yourselves something, believing that you are and exist, and act with strength and vigorous virtue, since it is certain that in order to abase one's-self one must be elevated and be something. A man who lowers himself or prostrates himself on the ground, must be standing or raised up; but he who lies all his length can no more abase himself, since he is in his last abasement. The more, then, that these souls think themselves abased by their humility-practice, which is, moreover, very good for a time, whilst the soul is yet incapable of anything else, the more they remain assured of their elevation; because the depth of the fall marks the height of the elevation, and also in their center it is a spiritual elevation that they subtlety seek in this humiliation. Thus the humility-practice, as a virtue, cannot enter into heaven, but it must pass into annihilation before it can be worthy of God, and filled with Himself and by Him alone. It is not so with these souls of whom I wish to speak. They can neither humiliate nor abase themselves, for the profundity of their lowness takes away all power of abasing themselves, having given up everything. Should they desire to do so, they would require to ascend on high, and thus issue out of their state. They are so persuaded that in order to humble themselves they would require to place themselves above what they are, that they do not see how they could ever desire it, or how any creature could possibly do it.

Truly it is only the Word-God who, by incarnating Himself, has lowered Himself below what He was, therefore Scripture says that He annihilated Himself (Phil. ii., v. 7), and which it says of no creature, not even of Mary. When Scripture speaks of Mary by the mouth of Mary herself; it says, that God hath regarded the profundity of her nothingness, but it does not say that she had annihilated herself, since she was properly a nothing; and Mary has been the most perfect of all creatures, only because she has been lower than any other in the depth of nothingness. The deeper this nothingness is, the more extended it is, and the more extended it is, the more perfect it becomes; and in proportion as this nothingness is deepened, the communication of God is made more abundant, so that Mary, not being able as a creature to go further into the profundity of nothingness, it was necessary that the divine Word should become incarnate in her, it being only the incarnation of the Word which could be a fullness corresponding to this profound annihilation.

For it must be known that the more profound the void is, God distributes Himself there with the greater extent; but as the goodness of God is infinite, He always bestows a superabundant fullness, as it is written, that His redemption has been most abundant and infinitely so (Rom. v., 15-20). Now it would have been necessary for Mary to have been God in order to have, by her annihilation, a void strictly proportioned to the fullness and replacement of the Word. Thus we may truly say that her replacement was most abundant and infinitely abundant, for her void was most profound and infinitely extended.

The proportion, however, between the void of Mary and the incarnation was this, that Mary, although bounded and limited as a creature, had reached the bottom of the whole extent of limited nothingness, and not all the extent of infinite nothingness which God alone can fathom.

To comprehend this it must be remarked that, although void and nothingness are, properly speaking, neither finite nor infinite, since they are nothing, and the privation of all being cannot possess the properties of being, yet they can be measured, in some manner, as to the beings of which they are the void and annihilation; and in a right sense we can say that there is more or less annihilation, according as there was or could be more being and exaltation. Thus, although the death of a prince and that of a slave are each only the privation of a human life, nevertheless that of the prince is much more annihilating than that of the slave, for it causes the loss of a much more noble life. This being laid down, I say that Mary having attained to the most profound nothingness as a creature, and the Word, as Word-God, having exhausted all the greatness of His Father by His perfect equality, without there remaining anything in the Father that does not pass into the Son, who exhausts to infinity the infinity of the Father; there was between Jesus and Mary this proportion (without proportion nevertheless), that Jesus had exhausted all greatness and all God, as Mary had exhausted all nothingness in the creature. This caused the Word, viewing this proportion of void with His fullness, to come and enclose Himself with all His greatness in Mary, it being only He who could fill her nothingness; but He filled it in a manner infinitely abundant.

I say then that it is not properly a perfect humility in the creature to humble itself; but to love its nothingness and to keep itself in it, leaving its God to do all that He desires, and believing that He can do it. Would it have been a humility for Mary to have refused to become the mother of God, and thus to place some difficulty in the way of accepting the divine incarnation? No assuredly, it would have been a subtle and secret pride, which would have led her to perform something by herself, or to excuse herself from what God desired of her. Attachment to humility cannot be a true humility, since it is contrary to pure charity, which ordains that the creature should not reserve to itself anything whatsoever, and that by a total dependence everything should be sacrificed to the sovereignty of God alone. Many err in this point, maintaining their humility by their self-will; and wanting in resignation and perfect renouncement of themselves, they offend divine charity, thinking that they favor humility, which nevertheless is not humility in what agrees not with charity. If light were granted to discern it, it would be clearly seen that where one believes he is humbling himself he is elevating himself; that in thinking to annihilate himself, he seeks his own subsistence; and that, in fine, one tastes and possesses the glory of humility, as a signal virtue, in the acts of humiliation that one practices.

The true nothingness does nothing and opposes nothing. It suffers itself to be conducted and led where it is desired; it believes that God can perform everything by it, (without regarding itself) just as He could do anything with a straw; and there is more humility in believing these things, and in giving one's-self up to them without laying hold of anything, than in excusing one's-self from them. Let us abandon ourselves with courage. If God does not do anything with us, He will render us justice, since we are good for nothing, and this will be His glory. If He performs great things in us, we shall say with Mary that "he has done great things in us, because he has regarded our lowness."

13. Neither is it beyond the sea, that thou shouldest complain saying, who amongst us can pass over

*the sea to bring it to us, that we might learn and
do what is commanded us.*

*14. But this word is very nigh unto thee; it is in thy
mouth, and in thy heart, that thou shouldst do it.*

*15. See, I set before thine eyes this day, life and
good; and on the contrary, death and evil,*

*16. That thou mayest love the Lord thy God, and
walk in His ways, adhering to him.*

17. Choose then life;—

20. For he is thy life.

Moses again shows how easy it is to follow this
road, saying that it *is* so *near us* that *this word* of life
(which discovers it to us) *is in our mouth and in our
heart,* and that *he has placed before our eyes death
and life, evil and good;* that we may love God; teaching us at the same time that the means of loving Him is
to make *a choice,* just and equitable, useful and advantageous.

This choice is to *adhere to God;* and this adherence stands for abandon and the entire conformity
of our will with His own: to *adhere* is not to do or to
move of one's-self; but to consent to what is done by
Him to whom we adhere. This adherence conducts the
soul to the highest perfection, as it is written, that "he
that adhereth unto God becomes of the same spirit with
him," (i Cor. vi. 17) because by the continuance of this
adherence he becomes uniform, even to being able no

more to see that he adheres, nor to force himself to hold himself attached, but he lives remaining united to the divine will. This is also remarked in this same Deuteronomy when it says "ye that adhere unto the Lord your God are all alive," (chap. iv. 4) without doubt from the life of Him to whom they are joined. And it is this very *adherence* which communicates to them this *life,* as it is also by it that God will perform in us what appears so difficult.

Chapter XXXI.

6. Take courage and be full of trust; fear not and be not afraid at the sight of thy enemies, for the Lord thy God himself will conduct thee, and he will not abandon thee nor forsake thee.

Scripture continues to exhort these souls never to excuse themselves from embracing a road so difficult to the creature that leans upon its self-strength, but so easy to God. *Take courage,* it says to them, and *be trustful.* This is not a thing that you are to undertake of yourselves, but *God* Himself *will be your conductor.* Abandon yourselves only to Him and He will never abandon you nor forsake you, even for a single moment. O advantage of abandon! The soul has nothing to do with taking care of itself nor giving itself any trouble about it. In abandoning itself to its God, He Himself conducts it. O sure conduct!

17. Surely it is because God is not with me that these evils have come upon me.

All *the evils* that *happen to* men come only *because God is not with them,* either on account of their having totally quitted Him through mortal sin, or because they withdraw themselves from Him for want of courage in remaining in the *abandon;* resuming themselves after having given themselves up. But so long as we persist in abandoning ourselves to God, there is nothing to be feared, and no evils can attack us.

> *23. The Lord gave these commands to Joshua, and said unto him, Be strong and of a good courage, for thou shalt bring the children of Israel into the land which I promised unto them, and I will be with thee.*

If strength is needed in souls to suffer themselves to be conducted fearlessly by a way which the greater part conceive all full of precipices, and the mind of man cannot comprehend, much more so is it needed in those persons who are to conduct others therein. Those have not only a particular assault to sustain, and to suffer the fears of their own destruction, but they must moreover bear the terrors and complaints of all the others whom God gives to them to make them enter and conduct them in so frightful deserts which, according to understanding and reason, even spiritually enlightened, are real losses and inevitable abysses. How often do even directors, becoming so convinced of their own destruction, fear extremely to destroy the others, and have lively apprehensions of it; although, when it is a question of giving advice when it is asked, they could not do other than persist in the impenetrable routes of the most naked faith and the blindest abandons? But receiving from heaven only responses of death to all assurance taken in the creature, as much for the others in this degree as for themselves, they must walk with their families in these frightsome deserts, and make their families walk there with them, by an impulse of the incomprehensible order of God, which leads them where they know not, and out of an apparent disorder makes for them the surest of all routes; and at the same time, the most inconceivable to man, for this is peculiar to abandoned souls who have not wished to set limits to their trust in God, nor to their sacrifice to all His will. It is just that He should exercise His rights and make them pass through all the trials which He has resolved to make of their fidelity.

Not only that, but these conductors of souls must bear all the blows discharged against the persons confided to them, and this is another extremely difficult thing. It happens usually that if a director is interior, all the demons and human persons league themselves against him; and not being able to find anything to reprehend in his morals, they tax his conducting, and wish to make him responsible for all the weakness and follies of those he conducts, which is truly an injustice, since all defects are personal; and if God, not to violate liberty, does not prevent souls from falling, often drawing more glory from their fall, because they are humbled by it, or through other secret but just judgments, how can people desire the director to be the guarantee of all the faults of those he directs? Was Judas badly led under the immediate and visible direction of Jesus Christ? *Was* not St. Peter the first among the apostles? Why then should people think it wrong that weaknesses should happen to some souls without the directors being responsible for them or blaming the way? So many thousands are seen to perish out of this way and nothing is said about them, yet if a single person commits a fault, which is perhaps only apparent herein, every one murmurs at it, and they attribute a shortcoming which is only personal, to the way or the direction.

To the director, then, great *courage* is necessary, and an extreme fidelity, not to leave off conducting these souls to the very end, in spite of these calumnies. Such a man may be assured that *God is with him.* Often even directors, seeing themselves greatly persecuted, lose courage and quit everything, thinking that everything is perishing in their hands, even until they are unfaithful enough to withdraw into solitude. I adjure them in the name of God never to do that; this is what the demon aims at by the persecutions he raises up against them, and they cause God to lose a very great glory which He would take in them, and in the persons they conduct; besides, they do themselves an inexplicable wrong, and are thus the cause of the ruin of a great number of souls, who for want of conducting never arrive at the prepared place. It could not be believed how much the demon gains by this; and it is for this he sets up so many batteries; he even makes use of good souls to succeed in it, leading them under false pretexts and pious intentions to declare themselves against the pure way, thinking they do God a service when they persecute His dearest friends. But God makes use of the same means *to fortify* by the cross

His faithful servants in His love, which does not hinder Him from often punishing their persecutors, and opening their eyes at last to His truth, to make them return to themselves.

Chapter XXXII.

1. Give ear O heavens to what I speak; and hear O earth the words of my mouth.

2. Let my doctrine spread as the rain, and my speech penetrate as the dew.

Moses sings a song unto the Lord. The singing of this song is known to very few, for it is necessary to be far advanced in God in order to express it.

This is the *new song* which is sung in heaven before the Lamb, and which was given to Moses at the end of his days in the flesh as a foretaste of that which he was to sing forever in glory. Blessed is he who receives this song, and who comprehends in some manner in his inmost this song which comes from God Himself, and which is sung in the soul, not by the soul; for it does nothing but receive and render back without ceasing the voice and words placed in it.

Although he renders to his God all glory and honor, he yet avows that all which proceeds *from his mouth* is great and fruitful. It is great, for it comes from God Himself; as *the rain* from heaven; and it is fruitful as *the dew,* rendering the earth fertile. Thus all *the words* of well-annihilated souls hit home and produce great fruits from their fertility.

> 2. *As thick rain upon the grass, and as showers upon the herb: for I will call upon the name of the Lord.*

The soul is in a state *to call upon the Lord* in a new manner; for it calls upon Him no longer for itself, but for His glory alone, powerless to appropriate anything whatsoever; thus its prayer is an extolling of the magnificence of God.

> 3. *Give homage to the greatness of our God.*

> 4. *The works of God are perfect, and all his ways are equitable.*

Moses feeling what was in himself, and seeing also what was in the people entrusted to him, cries: *How perfect is all that God does;* as if he meant in his transport, Why will not people suffer themselves to be conducted to God, since all that He does is so perfect, and imperfect works are only so because the creature puts its hand to them? He adds that *all his ways are just* and irreproachable, although they appear to the humanly wise as ways of folly, because they are founded on blind *abandon,* which excludes all reason and human power; but by trusting ourselves to God, and losing all self-prudence, we thus acquire all possible prudence. What greater prudence can there be than to resign our feebleness to so mighty a Protector, and to trust our treasure to so faithful a Friend whenever we see ourselves powerless to preserve it, or even certain to lose it if we wish to guard it ourselves, at least in very great danger?

> 4. *God is faithful and there is no injustice in Him.*
> *He is just and upright.*

It is to show the solidness of the judgment of those who trust themselves to God when it is said that *God is faithful and without injustice.* As faithful, He will never fail us, being true in His promises; and since He is *without injustice,* He cannot deceive us. This is even strengthened by what is added, that the Lord *is just and upright: as just,* He renders back with increase what we give up to Him; as *upright,* we have only to follow Him to walk in uprightness, for He is exempt from deceit.

> 5. *They have sinned against him, and are no longer*
> *his children, being defiled in their impurities.*
> *Wicked and perverse generation,*

> 6. *Foolish and senseless people, is it thus ye re-*
> *quite the Lord ?*

Moses, in his rapture of spirit, has no sooner made known to the people of Israel the advantage they have had in trusting to God, than in a spirit of prophecy he speaks against those who wandering from God merit no longer to be recognized as His children; and these are they who will not abandon themselves, or who, having already far advanced by the aid of the holy *abandon,* resume themselves at the time of the most severe and last trials. The broken language which he uses shows the elevation of his spirit in God; and what seems to be wanting in order is divinely ruled by the Holy Spirit, who speaks by the mouth of this great prophet.

He reproaches, then, *the depravity and folly* of these souls who will not abandon themselves to God.

Foolish and senseless people, he says to them, *is it thus ye requite the Lord?* As if he said to them, Why do ye make a difficulty in rendering all things in general to Him? Or why will you entrust Him with only a part of what you hold entirely from Him? This word *requite* is used to mark the restitution of all that we have from Him by gift: now, as it is certain that God has given us all that we are, we ought therefore to render unto Him all that we are; and this is done by the abandon of everything—riches, honors, life, body, soul, salvation, eternity, justice, holiness—in fine, all that composes our exterior and interior. Is it not to be bereft of our senses not to be willing to do this.

6. *Is not he your Father who has possessed you, who has made you, and created you?*

Is not God your Father? Is tenderness and love for you wanting in Him? Is it not He who ought to *possess you,* and do you not belong to Him already by so many just titles? Ought He not to regard you as His own property? And since He has had the power of *forming* you, will He not have that of preserving you, even to producing you anew if He desired? Even though you should be lost, could he not yet save you?

> *7. Remember the days of old. Recall to thy memory all the ages of the world. Ask thy father, and he will relate to thee what he has seen; ask thy elders, and they will tell thee what they have learned.*

Remember what you have known in *times past,* so that the experience of the bounties of God may increase your trust *Ask your fathers and elders* who have walked in these ways what has been their success. For although they appear to you only a frightful desert, and it seems to you that they must only end in eternal destruction, yet those who have happily arrived at the end of a career so long, so painful, and so obscure, will assure you that it terminates at nothing less than God Himself, who is found all alone at the end, by the happy loss of the creature into Him. Do not think that you are the only ones that walk in such frightsome roads; many persons have passed along them before you, and many others accompany you though you know them not. God exacts from His most faithful abandoned ones trials of naked faith and generous love proportioned to the greatness of the abandon He has placed in them. Be not astonished even if almost all the others seem to walk differently, for the steps of those who will walk themselves and see where they go, although leaning upon their Beloved, are different from the ways of those who let themselves be carried to their Love, blindly trusting to Him. Sustain yourselves a little upon the testimony *of the ancients,* until you can go to God alone by God Himself, without any other support.

8. When the Most High divided the nations, when he separated the children of Adam, he set the bounds of each people according to the number of the children of Israel.

9. But the portion of the Lord was his people, Jacob was the lot of his inheritance.

God from the beginning has *separated the children of Adam,* who conduct themselves, from His own children whom He has chosen to be *his people and portion.* Abandoned persons are blessed in being *the portion of God.* From the time when God becomes our sole portion, we also become His, whilst the others remain in part heirs of Adam, as Adam forms a good part of their inheritance; all is labor both for Adam and *his children;* all is *bounded* and limited for them; but all is repose for the Lord and His children; all is full of liberty, extent, and immensity for them.

10. He found him in a desert land, in a place of horror and vast solitude. He conducted him by long turnings, and instructed him, and preserved him as the apple of his eye.

But where *has* God *found this people;* and how has He known them to be his own? Oh it is *in the desert land,* in the total separation from all creatures, in the stripping of all good, in the privation of all support, in the *place of vast solitude, horrible* alike to nature and the spirit, where the soul finds itself all naked and alone, without being accompanied by anything whatsoever; ah, then it is that He *conducts it by long turnings and instructs it* in His purest will. *He guards it as the apple of his eye.* These words so well express God's care, and are so fit and proper, that we could not add anything to them without detracting somewhat from their beauty.

> *11. As an eagle stirreth up her young ones to fly, and fluttereth over them, he stretched forth his wings, and took him upon him, and bore him upon his shoulders.*

There is not a word in this verse but is ravishing. *As the eagle stirreth up her young ones to fly as she flies,* so God encourages as His children the abandoned souls to follow Him, to abandon themselves, to suffer themselves to be led, therefore He *flutters over them* like the eagle, to animate and encourage His little ones, to defend them, and to sustain them. It is by this fluttering that He gives them His spirit. He *stretches his wings* over them in the first place, to shelter them from the injuries of the time, from crosses, from persecutions, from the arrows of the devil and the flesh. He defends them from all peril, and covers them with His protection, *under the shadow of his wings;* but not content with that, for greater safety *he takes them upon him, and bears them upon his shoulders.*

Oh too fortunate souls! Elevated as you are upon this Royal Eagle, you look from on high upon all the other birds who fatigue themselves with flying, and who are always in danger of being taken by the kites, vultures, and other birds of prey, and who at most rise but a little way from the earth. But you, O fortunate young eagles, you border upon the heaven without it costing you anything! You rest yourselves, and you fly, and in this flight of full repose, you overtop all the heavens; and although you advance by immense sweeps, yet you are never fatigued, for even your advancement is a perfect repose, and the more peacefully you repose upon these shoulders of your heavenly Eagle the more you advance. Oh happiness beyond comprehension, but which may be fully experienced by giving and abandoning one's-self to God!

> *12. The Lord alone was his conductor, and there was no strange god with him.*

Whence comes the happiness of this soul—a happiness so unlooked for? It is that *God alone has been its conductor*, and He alone, and *no strange help with him*. O poor souls who fatigue yourselves in the multiplicity of your ways, if you knew the happiness of a soul which, without fatiguing itself; rests from all care of itself upon the arms of providence, you would be enraptured at it, and deplore the time you have lost without advancing, although walking with all your strength.

> *13. He established him upon a high and excellent land, to eat there the fruits of the fields, to suck honey out of the rock, and to draw oil from the flinty rock.*

The soul thus borne upon the wings of God, mounts upon a *land eminent* both by the height of its mountains, and *the excellence* of its fertility; that is to say, above everything created, be it earthly or heavenly. Above pure intelligences, faculties, and virtues, it passes beyond all, and goes to repose in God alone, where He conducts it Himself upon the wings of His providence and love. It is then that this soul *eats of the fruits of the field,* nourishing itself no longer, but with the most exquisite things—God and His Holy Will. The will of God is *the fruit* of all lands, for all pains which are borne in the other ways are only to arrive at the knowledge and fulfillment of the will of God; but this soul *eats* of the fruits without any more cultivating them, being itself transformed and established permanently in the will of God, without power to come out of it except by an infidelity like to that of Lucifer.

It also *sucks* there *honey out of the rock.* This honey from the rock marks, in this soul, the good qualities of the rock, namely, firmness, hardness, insensibility, and immovability. This soul then is made firm as a rock in the will of God, it has also the hardness of it, for neither all arrows nor blows can make any impression, and are all broken at its feet without piercing it. It is, moreover, insensible to all things corporeal, human, and spiritual, and in fine immovable as a *rock,* so that all the attacks of hell cannot stir it or make it change its state. Behold what it is to suck honey out of the rock. Finally, it *draws* oil from the flinty rock, in that although it is thus firm, hard, immovable, and insensible to every thing, and made firm in the will of God, in which it is invariable, there flows however from this rock an *oil* and heavenly balm, which without this rock feeling aught of it, yet penetrates all that approaches it, and distributes itself efficaciously in the hearts which God sends to it.

> *15. This well-beloved people became fat and re-belled; after being well nourished, fattened, and enriched, they have quitted God, their Creator, and withdrawn from God their Savior.*

This whole song is interspersed with interruptions, and broken with transports. After Moses has depicted the fortunate souls who have entered into the nakedness of the desert, and have suffered themselves to be borne to God, he describes the state of those who are conducted by lights and relishes which he calls *becoming fat.* The first have only been carried by God because they were entirely denuded, and the latter, who appear the well-beloved and most cherished, have quitted God only because they were very *fat.* This is clear. *They have become fat,* and afterwards *have elevated themselves.* This is the property of the state of the illuminative life, and of the passivity of light, to fatten the soul by a certain fullness which it communicates to it; and then the soul begins to elevate itself, finding itself, as it seems to it, in a more perfect state than any other, so that being full, it reposes in its fullness, which is as the fat and filling up of the three faculties of the soul—the understanding, the will, and the memory—and seeing nothing better, it fancies itself at the end of its course.

Those in this state have much assurance of their salvation, and the goodness of their state leaves them almost no doubt of it. Whence there happen to them two things—first, that they attribute so many graces to their fidelity, leading them to despise the others, who appear more imperfect, although really they are further advanced if they are of the true denuded ones; and thus they forget that it is God who has done this by His pure goodness without any merit on their part. Secondly, reposing in the gifts of God, of which they are full, they forget to run to God alone, and go beyond all gifts to find Himself, so that their very abundance of the gifts of God is to them the occasion of *quitting God,* by the bad use they make of them, and the proprietary attachment they have to them. These persons, who are thus in light, yet continue to be wellbeloved of God even to the end (although in a manner very different from the others), God bestowing on them a thousand caresses, for gifts and graces are not incompatible with propriety when it is not a mortal sin; but God alone cannot be found therein, and He gives Himself only to the soul which, in the frightful wilderness, has lost all propriety and support.

18. Ye have abandoned the God who made you, and have forgotten the Lord who created you.

God all full of love and goodness for these souls yet cannot forbear thus lovingly reproaching them— *What! ye have abandoned the God who made* you; ye have quitted the end for the means; ye have stopped at the gifts and left the Giver; ye have lain down at the pleasantest spot on your journey instead of ascending up to your origin! It must be observed that although God bestows so many graces upon these feeble souls, He does so only with some regret, and on account of their weakness, depriving Himself of the great glory and infinite pleasure which He would have had if these souls, by generously despising all these riches, should go beyond them all to mount up to Him who created them, and to return like rivers into the sea whence they derive their origin.

> *19. And when the Lord saw that, his anger was kindled because his sons and daughters provoked him.*

> *20. And he said, I will hide my face from them, and will see what their end shall be.*

The Lord, not wishing to lose these proprietary and interested souls, leaves them His gifts, knowing that without them they would perish. *He sees it, however, and his anger is kindled at it,* protesting moreover that since they act thus they will never arrive in this life at their *final end,* which is to enjoy God Himself and not His gifts; therefore, He adds, *I will hide my face from them,* that is to say, they shall remain deprived of the possession of their Sovereign Good, since they have preferred things of so little value to Me. This is also pointed out in what follows.

> *21. They have provoked my wrath in that which was not God.*

Wishing to possess what is *less than God,* they have been deprived of the possession of God Himself. Oh inestimable loss!

39. Know ye that I am alone, and there is no other God than I. I kill and I make alive; I wound and I heal; and none can escape from my hand.

This verse teaches us further how much God desires us to be abandoned to Him alone, and to lean on nothing out of Him. It is as if He said, since *ye know that I am alone,* and that there is nothing like to Me, I desire likewise to be alone in you in all that I do there. Who is able to do that which I do? Is there another God than I? It is I alone who can *make* souls *die* to themselves, and no labor of the creature can accomplish it; and it is I alone who can *restore their life,* and after having killed them, resuscitate and make them alive again.

Tell us, Oh Love-God! What inventions hast Thou wherewith to wound Thy most faithful lovers? Ah! how little would they be comprehended by mortal men, even though Thou shouldst tell us them. Thou *woundest them,* Thou sayest, and Thou *healest* them. Oh how deep are those wounds! It is Thou who smitest, and at the same time thou hidest Thyself; and Thou leavest only the pain of the wounds Thou hast made. The soul thus wounded thinks it can never be healed; it defends itself as long as it can from Thy blows; it doubts even if they are from Thee; and when it is Thou who smitest it, it complains to Thyself of the blows Thou givest, as if they came from another, for it knows not that Thou smitest it. Oh if it knew that it was Thou who smitest it it would be too happy, and would reckon as its delights its most cruel wounds! But alas! Thou hidest Thyself; and Thy lover thus wounded cries and bewails bitterly; it thinks that because it is thus disfigured and covered with wounds Thou no longer lovest it; and the horror of its wounds leads it to wish evil to itself; thinking that they have happened to it by its own fault, and that if it had well defended itself this invincible hand would not thus have disfigured it. Console thyself, poor loving one, console thyself; thou knowest not who is thy innocent murderer. If thou didst know it, thou wouldst esteem thyself more happy in being killed by His hand, than to be made alive by any other.

But what does He, this amiable cruel one? *He heals* all the wounds which He Himself has given. For it must be observed that none but He can heal the ills He sends. He heals then His loving one, and that with so much pleasure that it would wish no other thing than to be wounded thus, to have the pleasure of being healed again. God hides Himself when striking, but allows Himself to be seen when He heals, so that the soul knows not for a long time that it is He who has wounded it, yet it cannot be ignorant of His healing it.

But why, Oh Lord, dost Thou heal this soul with so much care? Is it not a species of cruelty, since Thou only healest it to wound it the more deeply, and to kill it altogether? Yes dear souls, this cure which appears so delightful to you must cost you your life. Ah! What a different pain this will be for you. The pain of death is quite different from that of a wound: and when the death blow is given, you will also not know who it is that killeth you.

The poor soul is so blind, that it thinks it is itself that has buried the poignard in its bosom. No, no; *it is* the unknown *who kills* you: and as He has wounded you only to heal you, He kills you only to *make* you *alive* again, but with a life quite different from the one you had before, which was rather a continual death, since you lived only to die; in place of this you die only to live for ever in a new and permanent life. Defend yourselves as long as you please, your defenses will only cause your punishment to be prolonged, as He says Himself that *none shall escape from his hand.* No, no; all your efforts will be useless. You can make them if you like, but it is certain that you cannot escape death.

> *40. I will lift up my hand to heaven and say, It is I who live for ever.*

These words relating to what has been already said, point out that God kills this soul only because it has a life contrary to His own, this *lifting of his hand* being as it were an oath which He takes; as if He said, I swear the death of this soul because it still lives in itself, and it is necessary that *I live only:* but that I may do so, I must annihilate everything living in it that is opposed to my sole life, and when that is done *I shall live* in it *for ever.*

> *42. I will make my arrows drunk with blood, and my sword shall devour the flesh of the blood of those I have slain, and the enemies with bare heads, and those I have taken captive.*

God is not content with killing this soul, as has been said He pursues it yet after its death to annihilate it, so that there may remain nothing of it. Therefore He says that *he will make his arrows drunk with its blood;* as if he said, By dint of smiting it my arrows will become all filled, soaked, and drunk with blood. This is not all: I wish not only that there remain no more blood to this creature, that is to *say,* no principle of life in it, as it is said in Lev. xvii. 14, *"the soul of the living flesh is in its blood,"* and it was on that account the Israelites were forbidden to eat blood, the source of the self-life being then in the blood, not only must there remain no more of it, but the sword of the Lord *will* afterwards *devour* the very *flesh of the blood,* the flesh formed by the blood and nourished by it. It is not said that His sword will cut this flesh, but that it will devour it, thus denoting annihilation. This flesh is the flesh of the blood. This expression is admirable. God does not say the blood of the flesh, for the blood usually issues from the flesh, but *the flesh of the blood,* to show that He means by that everything appertaining to the self-life. The first is that of the flesh; therefore blood must be drawn from the flesh to weaken it; and this life is the life of sin, which is quitted when one is converted. But this other life which must perish here, is the spiritual life, and the life of the soul, denoted by the blood. Now this life in such souls issues *from the blood;* for although it is a life of spirit and grace, yet it has become a little carnal, and mingled with the flesh by propriety. But this flesh is no longer the reservoir of the blood, where it dwells in a continual and abundant manner, it is only the appendage and remains of it, therefore God by His sword devours this flesh, so that there remains no more of it. The arrows are indeed drunken with blood, but they do not devour it wholly, the sword must finish by consuming *the flesh of this blood.*

But of what blood? The blood of those already dead, as it is written, *the blood of those I have slain.* It is not sufficient to be dead, it is moreover necessary to be annihilated, and also captivity must be destroyed, as it is said of Jesus Christ, that "ascending into heaven he led captivity captive." This captivity is a certain contracting of the soul, hindering its expansion, as it has been said, and which can only be taken away by annihilation. Now this captivity was *from the naked chief of our enemies.* The chief of our enemies is propriety: this propriety had been wholly stripped by death: but there yet remained a certain restriction, rendering the soul captive, because it prevented it from being extended, and it is this that is achieved by the devouring of annihilation.

CHAPTER XXXIII.

2. The Lord is come to Sinai, and has risen up from Seir upon us. He has appeared upon Mount Paran, and thousands of saints were with him. He holds in his right hand a law of fire.

The Lord is come to the mountain, which is His throne, and His throne is no other than Himself. He has come from two sides; from *Sinai,* mount of graces, of light and love; but *he has risen from Seir, a* desert place, and appeared *upon Mount Paran* by a new communication of His graces. *Thousands of saints are with him,* the spirits of the blessed and the annihilated souls. These blessed spirits are very holy, for there is nothing in them but what is of God; thus they are always with Him, for they are holy only from Him. This also marks the magnificence of God, who never comes alone into a soul, but accompanied by an infinity of gifts and graces, and a profusion of heavenly favors, so much the more sublime as they appear less so, and so much the more pure as they are in Himself, and not in the proper capacity of the creature: thus these thousands of angels who accompanied Him upon Mount Sinai were most intimately and for ever united to Him.

The Lord *holds in his right hand a law of fire.* This fiery law is charity, which must consume and annihilate all that there is in man as of man; for as long as there remains something of it, he cannot be holy. It is this law of fire which makes the saints; and no saint can be holy without passing through it. This fiery law burns the heart, and reduces to ashes all self-love, to leave there only pure love.

> *3. He has loved the people: all the saints are in his hands, and all those that approach his feet will receive his doctrine.*

God *loves* all *the people,* that is, all the faithful, but it is properly only *the saints* who *are in his hands.* These are the abandoned souls who allow themselves to be moved at His will. They are in His hands for Him to do all that He pleaseth with them. *And those who approach his feet;* those who are nearest and most supple, and whose annihilation has made them His footstool (for God walks over abysses), these are they who *will receive his doctrine* and truth, and who will be instructed in His secrets the most hidden from others, beholding the economy of His providence, penetrating His supreme will above all things, and admiring how it is discovered to the little souls.

Moses admirably comprehends, in these few words, the entrance, progress, and infinite fruits of contemplation and the passive way. God, he says, has loved His people. When *love* advances reciprocally between God and the creature, it renders the souls *holy,* and from the time when they begin to be holy, they also begin to be passive: abandoning themselves with the more generosity, and leaving themselves *in God's hands,* both increase proportionately. The more a heart is holy, the more it is abandoned, and the more abandoned it is, the more it is holy, since holiness cannot be found out of God. This is well expressed when it is said that *all the saints are in God's hands.* He who says all excepts none, whence it is also clear that the more we excuse ourselves from the holy abandon, the further we remove ourselves from holiness, since we wish not to cast ourselves into God's hands, but to lean upon our own, and, as it were, walk upon them; and on the contrary, the most infallible means of soon arriving at holiness is to cast ourselves as speedily as possible into the arms of God, which is no other thing than to trust ourselves blindly to God, and to submit ourselves unreservedly to His will, which is the foundation and rule of all holiness.

But when Moses adds, that all those who approach the feet of the Lord will learn his doctrine, might it not be said that he depicts Mary at the feet of the Savior, where she listens to His speech, and with her all the contemplatives of which she is the example and figure? As all those who remain in repose at the feet of the Lord infallibly learn His doctrine, for listening to Him, they give Him room to teach them; those, on the contrary, who do not enter into this repose will never learn the doctrine of the Lord, since wishing always to speak before Him, and never to listen to Him, they suffer Him not to instruct them; as also stirring unceasingly by continual and violent agitations of their senses and faculties, they leave Him no freedom to unite them to Himself. God being all repose, it is necessary to remain in repose in order to be united to Him; and since His Word is all speech, it is necessary to be all silence to hear Him, and all ear to receive Him. Moses wishes, then, to teach us that it is necessary to be silent, to repose, and to listen, to leave room for the generation of the Word in the soul, which is properly *to receive the doctrine of the Lord,* for the Word is the doctrine of the Father.

> *7. Hear, Lord, the voice of Judah, and bring him with his people. His hands will fight for Israel, and he will be their protector against their enemies.*

Judah has always been taken for Jesus Christ; therefore the blessing given to this tribe differs from the others. It is uttered in the form of a prayer addressed to God in the name of Judah, that is to say, in the name of Jesus Christ, who prays his Father to bring him with his people into the land of eternal salvation, which is to be given through him to his chosen ones, and to establish him its liberator and defender.

> *9. Levi said unto his father and to his mother, I know you not, and to his brethren, I do not know you, nor have they known their own children. They have kept thy word, and they have observed thy covenant.*

The tribe of Levi has always been that of advanced souls, chosen to conduct others, therefore they know no person according to the flesh, neither *father, mother, brethren, nor children,* being stripped of everything natural and human, and all productions and proprieties. These faithful directors have no longer any consideration hindering them from doing the will of God. Thus it is said, that *they faithfully keep all his words, and observe his covenant.* This covenant is no other than abandon; by which the soul, giving itself wholly to God to do His will, God also treats with it, assuring it that He will conduct it Himself and make it do His will, if it remain abandoned to His guidance. Is not this a treaty of alliance by which the creature gives itself freely to its God, and God promises it His protection, and to be its surety in all things? To observe His covenant is to remain in destitution.

CHAPTER XXXIV.

10. There was not seen a prophet since in all Israel like unto Moses, whom the Lord knew face to face.

It is so rare a thing to find a man so far advanced as Moses, fit to conduct souls to the last degree of their consummation, that Scripture has even acknowledged it. *There are found* almost *none* who enter into God in so perfect a manner, which is, *to see him face to face* (that is to say, without medium, without support, propriety, or any thing mediate), because of the difficulty men have, and above all, men of some knowledge and reputation, to suffer themselves to be denuded, as it is necessary for the mystic death and annihilation, by which alone it is possible to pass into God.

SeedSowers
P.O. Box 3317
Jacksonville, FL 32206
800-228-2665
904-598-3456 (fax)   www.seedsowers.com

THE CHRONICLES OF THE DOOR *(Edwards)*

The Beginning 8.99
The Escape 8.99
The Birth 8.99
The Triumph 8.99
The Return 8.99

THE WORKS OF T. AUSTIN-SPARKS

The Centrality of Jesus Christ 19.95
The House of God 29.95
Ministry 29.95
Service 19.95
Spiritual Foundations 29.95
The Things of the Spirit 10.95
Prayer 14.95
The On-High Calling 10.95
Rivers of Living Water 8.95
The Power of His Resurrection 8.95

COMFORT AND HEALING

A Tale of Three Kings *(Edwards)* 8.99
The Prisoner in the Third Cell *(Edwards)* 5.99
Letters to a Devastated Christian *(Edwards)* 5.95
Healing for those who have been Crucified by Christians *(Edwards)* 8.95
Dear Lillian *(Edwards)* 5.95

OTHER BOOKS ON CHURCH LIFE

Climb the Highest Mountain *(Edwards)* 9.95
The Torch of the Testimony *(Kennedy)* 14.95
The Passing of the Torch *(Chen)* 9.95
Going to Church in the First Century *(Banks)* 5.95
When the Church was Young *(Loosley)* 8.95
Church Unity *(Litzman, Nee, Edwards)* 14.95
Let's Return to Christian Unity *(Kurosaki)* 14.95

CHRISTIAN LIVING

The Autobiography of Jeanne Guyon 14.95
Final Steps in Christian Maturity *(Guyon)* 12.95
Turkeys and Eagles *(Lord)* 8.95
The Life of Jeanne Guyon *(T.C. Upham)* 17.95
Life's Ultimate Privilege *(Fromke)* 10.00
Unto Full Stature *(Fromke)* 10.00
All and Only *(Kilpatrick)* 7.95
Adoration *(Kilpatrick)* 8.95
Release of the Spirit *(Nee)* 6.00
Bone of His Bone *(Huegel)* modernized 8.95
Christ as All in All *(Haller)* 9.95